FOUND IN JESUS

NOT LOST IN MOTHERHOOD

This Book is Given To:

_____

With Love From:

_____

Date:

_____

Book One

THE FOUND MAMA

30-DAY DEVOTIONAL & PRAYER JOURNAL ON IDENTITY IN JESUS

KRISTINA BROOKS

Path Publishing
HOUSE

Published by Path Publishing House

For information, please visit www.authorkristinabrooks.com or send e-mail correspondence to authorkristinabrooks@gmail.com.

ISBN 979-8-9913697-1-8

Dedication

For my Momma, who's life answers the question, "why does being a godly mother matter?" How beautiful it is to be just one of many women in our family who were raised by believers and set out to raise more believers. Thank you for continuing this legacy. Thank you for never giving up on me. I love you, I admire you, and I am so proud to be your daughter.

Found in
Jesus,
Not Lost in
Motherhood

Contents

Foreword   1
Introduction   5
Day 1: Lost in Motherhood is a Lie   11
Day 2: Why is Motherhood Difficult?   17
Day 3: In a World Selling Lost   22
Day 4: Found Fighting   28
Day 5: Mamas Know Milk   34
Day 6: Good Things A-Spillin'   39
Day 7: God Hears Our Prayers   45
Day 8: After He Answers the Prayer   49
Day 9: Accepting a Lot   57
Day 10: The Found Mama   67
Day 11: Found in Jesus   75
Day 12: Choosing Sin   82
Day 13: Having it All Together   89
Day 14: Authentic Motherhood   97
Day 15: Realistic Expectations   103
Day 16: Found Wonderfully Made   110
Day 17: Avoiding Burn Out   119
Day 18: The Good Ol' Days   129
Day 19: Found Faithful   133
Day 20: Found Still   139
Day 21: Found Frustrated   148
Day 22: The Coffee Tastes Better When He Makes It 154
Day 23: Making Memories   159
Day 24: Hard Things   165
Day 25: Mom Tired   170
Day 26: Wasting Time   178
Day 27: Like God Sent You   184
Day 28: All of Me   190
Day 29: How To Be a Christian Mom   197
Day 30: Losing My Mind   204
Acknowledgements   i
Free Digital Download   v
About the Author   vi

Foreword

"I'd let her rear my children."

You have to understand how I feel about my children to understand and appreciate those words.

My daughters are my treasures. They are my blessings.

While they were still in my womb, in a conversation with God I said a prayer along the lines, "I know they are lent to me. I know they are ultimately yours. And while they are entrusted in my care I will, with a grateful heart, remember they are Yours."

The words from Deuteronomy 6:7 KJV, "And thou shalt teach them [the words of God] diligently unto thy children, and shalt talk of them when thou sittest in thine house, and when thou walkest by the way, and when thou liest down, and when thou risest up"; they were my daily touchstone.

I would not take lightly who I would trust to rear my children "in the nurture and admonition of the Lord" (Ephesians 6:4 KJV). Very, very few would qualify.

To clarify, my children aren't much younger than Kristina. Does that make my previous statement silly or ridiculous?

It does not.

I know who my girls have become. I know who they have trusted and "in whom they have believed" (2 Timothy 1:12). I know the joy of being the mother of two women who unapologetically proclaim Jesus Lord over their lives.

It makes my statement that much more valid.

If Kristina and I were contemporaries, to whom would I have entrusted my children? To whom would I have faith that they would do all they could do to deliver them to the same place of devotion? To whom would I hope would introduce them to the One who is the Jehovah-Shalom?

I would want to entrust them to someone who loves God well, studies and loves His word greatly. I would want someone who is Holy Spirit led and whose desire is to see Jesus shine in her life and the lives of her children. That's who I would trust.

Kristina is trustworthy and transparent.

She is transparent enough to share her confusion, but her story doesn't end there. Jesus came into her story and while she was seeking answers, Jesus was seeking to give her peace.

Most of all, I trust in Whom she found her answers. Her trust isn't in her wisdom, it's in the Savior who answered her questions.

When you read her book, you will get to see and know her.

She sits behind me in church. I've watched her family grow. I was at her home for her wedding reception, at the hospital when her son was born, and across the aisle at her daughter's baby dedication.

I wish you could meet her face to face.

She is lovely. She really is just who you meet on her Instagram feed. She has more gears turning at any one moment that I could possibly count. Yet, there is so little confusion in her world. Chaotic energy in her lively home, yes! But also, real peace.

In a world of discord and confusion, I am so grateful my friend dwells under the Prince of Peace's domain, and lives life abundantly within His boundaries and His blessings.

If you have picked up this book, I suspect you want this for you and your children as well.

Moms, we are entrusted with treasures.

Moms, you are treasures as well.

In the eyes of Jesus, you are a treasure. In the eyes of Kristina, you are a treasure.

Jesus wants you and your little ones to find peace inside His plan and the ultimate joy that comes from His plan. Jesus wants this for you and for your children and your children's children.

Kristina's heart is to bless you with the truth she has found from a life rescued. Her heart is fixed on blessing you with the assurances God has cemented in her own spirit. She wants to refresh you, Mama, with the wells that have sustained and nurtured her soul.

May the Prince of Peace capture You and keep you and Your Treasures within the walls of His kingdom of peace forever and ever. Amen

Mrs. Karyn
avid reader, run-on sentence eliminator, delighted friend, avatar dance partner, and huge fan

Introduction

Motherhood is a gift from God, but I did not always feel that way or recognize that truth.

When I first found out that I was going to be a mother, I was beyond scared. I was devastated. My husband and I *never* planned to have children. But God had a different plan.

When God has a plan – even if it's one that you never saw coming – you may find yourself feeling more than a little lost. We surely did!

Jesus not only saves the lost, but He keeps showing up and showing us His plan. Sometimes His plans are surprising and sometimes unsettling, but always perfect.

Can I tell you something important, something I desperately needed to know myself?

You were *chosen* by the creator of the universe to become a mother to your specific child or children. God knew everything about you and everything your children would come to be, and He still chose you. It was a gift, and it was an intentional one.

And yet, we are in a broken, ugly, fallen world where sharing memes on social media that say things like "I lost myself when I became a mom," is the norm. What is more common to witness - a mama complaining about motherhood or praising God for all that motherhood encompasses (even the mundane, even the hard)?

I, too, have lived in those moments where I felt lost. I felt like I was miles away from the old me, from my old life. One of the core memories I associate with that feeling was when I transformed my art studio into a playroom. I sold things off, boxed up paint and supplies, and made donation piles. A part of my life, a part of *me* that once took up a whole room in our house, was reduced to a single cabinet in our bathroom! The truth is, we all give up things that we love when we become mamas. The reasons behind these changes may vary, as do the sacrifices themselves, but once motherhood begins, it has a way of taking over your heart and life and pushing things aside, even if only for a season.

Parenting is hard. A thousand decisions a day based on what's best for someone else is hard. Somedays you feel like you lost – you.

But let's hold on a minute--- are we really declaring over our lives that we *lost* our identity?! Is that even possible? Our identity should be rooted in Christ to begin with, and to say we lost it to motherhood, to a gift that the Lord gave us ... something about that doesn't add up.

But when other people say it, when we hear other moms talking about how they don't do the things they used to do before they had kids, and we hear other moms sharing about how their hobbies are nonexistent or their identity is all wrapped up in caring for their families and they're burned out and tired and all they want is some me time *and it all sounds so relatable*. We are left with this little tingling feeling of dissatisfaction that whispers to the soul, "maybe I'm lost, too."

Ask yourself this question:

> *Why are so many moms saying that they are lost and why does it feel so relatable?*

Relatable things don't mean that they're the way God wants us to feel.

That's not to say we aren't allowed to feel the way we feel, but I am telling you that we don't have to set up camp everywhere that feels a little cozy and familiar and proclaim it over our lives as the gospel truth.

I don't know how you feel day in and day out.

I don't know what your struggles are, and you don't know mine. We might have very similar lives, or we might have lives that are as different as two lives could ever be from one another.

I don't know where you are in your motherhood journey, but I do know that life is hard and motherhood is hard, and I never want to tell anyone how they should or shouldn't feel. What I *do* want to do is remind us – you and me – that Jesus came so that we would never have to be lost again.

I named this series of books *The Found Mama* in response to the "I lost myself in motherhood" mentality that is so prevalent in our society today. Instead of focusing on the things we lost in motherhood, my book helps us focus on being found – found obedient, found faithful, found joyful, found busy in our calling to motherhood, found in the presence of the Lord.

We are the found mamas because we are found in Jesus, not lost in motherhood.

We are the found mamas, and my prayer for you is that by the end of this book, you will know that to be true with all of your heart.

One last thing.

A dear friend of mine once sent me a devotional to read. And it was ... porridge, just right! It made me excited about reading the Bible and spending time with God. Spending time with God and His word became easier, more comfortable, and that allowed it to be even more fulfilling.

In a way, it led me here.

It is my desire for you to have a similar experience and maybe even be the friend that passes that experience on to another mama, sister, or friend. My prayer is you will find spending time with God and His word a place of comfort.

You will experience the "just right-ness" of those moments.

And now, without further ado, welcome to The Found Mama Club.

I Am A Found Mama

Found in
Jesus,
Not Lost in
Motherhood

Day 1:

Lost in Motherhood is a Lie

1 Peter 5: 7-10 NLT

Give all your worries and cares to God, for he cares about you. Stay alert! Watch out for your great enemy, the devil. He prowls around like a roaring lion, looking for someone to devour. Stand firm against him, and be strong in your faith. Remember that your family of believers all over the world is going through the same kind of suffering you are. In his kindness God called you to share in his eternal glory by means of Christ Jesus. So after you have suffered a little while, he will restore, support, and strengthen you, and he will place you on a firm foundation.

The idea that we can lose ourselves in motherhood is a lie from the devil and it's a good one, because we've all believed it at one point or another. Not only that, but it's a lie that can completely devour every good thing about our motherhood experience and spit out the bones.

The power of suggestion can be so strong. Have you ever noticed that?

When I was pregnant with my son, I didn't have your typical or cliché pregnancy cravings like pickles and ice cream. But I did have cravings. I would experience intense, *intense* cravings for whatever I saw a commercial for on tv. If we were watching a show and someone was eating a hotdog, I needed a hotdog right then. I saw a commercial for popcorn, and this little mama (who doesn't even like popcorn) ran out and bought an entire family sized box of popcorn because just the suggestion of popcorn being good suddenly felt like a requirement for my continued existence. The power of suggestion. Similarly, there's this running joke in our family that I could sell my husband his own kidney because the power of suggestion really does a number on him sometimes.

Don't you think our enemy knows this about our human nature, knows that sometimes just the idea of something is enough to send us over the edge?

Did you read our key verses for today?

We *do* have a very real enemy who wants nothing more than to completely devour us and he has many tactics, like the lie that we've all somehow lost a little bit of ourselves in motherhood.

That lie isn't the thing that's meant to bring us into this sisterhood of moms.

We should unite over far better things. because there's more to this journey than echoing "me too" when someone says they feel a little lost. I propose that we find our common thread in the truth that we *aren't* lost because Jesus says He came to find us. That's where the sisterhood should be – that despite the hard parts of motherhood, we serve a risen Savior who makes us strong. What a difference it makes to join in with a group of women who rise up and say "it's hard, but I'm standing firm in the faith" instead of tying ourselves to the group of women who declare that motherhood has devoured them.

Motherhood? Devouring? No.

The Bible says the *enemy* devours and we are going to be more intentional about resisting him and all his schemes.

Start today by asking God to hide these verses in your heart because it is beautiful and encouraging and smart, and *this is our strategy* for life.

Take a deep breath as your read our verses for today again, settling in on the words that God cares about you. Stand a little taller as you're encouraged by the Scriptures. Widen your eyes a bit at the instruction to be alert. Thoughtfully consider the tactics our enemy on the prowl might use to devour us.

Do you really believe that it is outside the realm of possibility that the devil could use social media to weasel discontented thoughts into our subconscious? He is willing to do anything to destroy us, and those arrows being shot at us aren't always brightly flaming and obvious.

Feel powerful as you read these words of strength and encouragement.

Spending time with God is *how* we can stand firm in our faith. Take comfort in knowing that you aren't alone in your suffering – people all over the world are under attack from the same enemy, dealing with the same issues. No matter how easy it is to get lost in our sorrows and struggles, the Bible says you are not alone. Other people are going through things like this, too.

Other mamas, maybe even some who are reading this book, are going through the motherhood struggles right beside you. Picture us in your mind's eye. We are your sisters!

And now picture the God of all grace. The God who put you right where He put you, has called you to a life and a purpose for good. He has called you into the ministry that is motherhood. He has also called you to one day join Him in Heaven, but first — we will have this suffering. Sin entered the world a long time ago and this is just our reality; the Bible tells us this! Don't expect an unrealistically perfect life when the Bible clearly tells us we will suffer. (I'm guilty of this, too.)

Take heart and dig deep and pray to God for the strength to go on when you feel like you can't. We know who wins the war. One day, we will be restored. One day it will all be made perfect. You are not lost. You are found, mama.

Prayer Journal Prompt

Lord, help me to see the devil's lies for what they are – lies meant to keep me from You, from other Christians, and from the life You have planned for me. I have believed that I've lost myself in motherhood, but now I see that with Your help, I don't have to feel that way. I need help resisting

...

Day 2:

Why is Motherhood Difficult?

Ephesians 6:12 NLT

For we are not fighting against flesh-and-blood enemies, but against evil rulers and authorities of the unseen world, against mighty powers in this dark world, and against evil spirits in the heavenly places.

Motherhood is hard and it is so easy to feel discouraged, and we all know it! But have you ever really considered *why*?

Mama, you have a very real enemy out there. He's the same enemy I have. He prowls around, like we learned yesterday, and let's not take the word "prowl" lightly – this is serious. Literally, life and death are at stake.

The devil seeks to destroy everything good in our lives, and one of his biggest targets is the family. Mama, you have a target on your back and a mastermind sniper aiming for you. Motherhood is hard because God has given us the very important job of raising our babies to know and follow the King – and the Prince of Darkness is out to derail that plan by whatever means necessary. You aren't struggling against yourself, against your kids, or anything else.

Look at our key verse from today - we struggle against darkness.

The lie "I lost myself in motherhood" is one such form of darkness. It's a lie manufactured by Satan, have no doubt. But it's been picked up, adopted, and carried out in countless ways, like a cancer attacking the body. Who can blame him? We're easy targets.

> *Motherhood is hard because God has given us the very important job of raising our babies to know and follow the King — and the Prince of Darkness is out to derail that plan by whatever means necessary.*

Why are we easy targets?

We have a lot on our plates and we're tired.

Satan wants us weak.

When we are weak, our families are weak.

When we are tired - perhaps too tired to spend time with God and too tired to cover our families in prayer, and too tired to make church a priority in our lives - that gives the very real enemy more room to work out his devilish schemes.

If he can weasel his way in and prevent any amount of goodness, purity, or godliness from ever taking root, then he won't have to work as hard to overcome the relationships with God.

Motherhood is hard because Satan wants us discouraged, not in line with God, and not raising Christian families. He works against our every move. But God is for us, and the victory is His and we know who wins the war.

However, diligence falls on our shoulders.

It can feel like just another thing to do, I get it. But spending time to get in alignment with God daily is one of those "things to do "that helps everything else fall into place.

We'll keep talking about it, but I want you to really start looking at the concept of losing yourself in motherhood as a lie from Satan meant to destroy you, destroy your family, destroy your peace and joy, and to keep you feeling damaged.

For every lie, there is an opposite truth, and maybe if you've been feeling lost in motherhood, it's going to be particularly difficult for you to set that mentality aside without picking something else up in return. Try this on for size. You can't get lost when you're following Jesus.

It's time to pick ourselves up, tell Satan we don't believe his lies anymore, and ask God to protect us against and give us discernment to recognize these lies and schemes.

This is the first step to making motherhood feel a little easier.

This is the first step in feeling *found* again.

Prayer Journal Prompt

God, reveal to me any lies from the devil that I've accepted as truth. Will you please give me more wisdom and the discernment to recognize his schemes quickly? You are the Good Father, and You alone can protect me and my family from danger and destruction. One of the hardest parts of motherhood for me is ...

Day 3:

In a World Selling Lost

Luke 19:10 NLT

For the Son of Man came to seek and save those who are lost.

Have you ever let anyone make you feel less-than?

This can be anything, but I'll give you a few examples. Have you ever walked away from a conversation with someone, and you felt worse about yourself and your life than you did before you talked to them? Have you ever watched a movie or tv show and when you sat down, you thought you were happy, but when you got up, you felt like maybe your life wasn't as great as you thought it was? Have you ever noticed an advertisement selling a solution to a problem you didn't know you had until you were suddenly aware of it?

Yesterday, we talked about resisting our very real enemy, and today we're going to look at something a little more uncomfortable. In much of our world, the enemy rules. It can be easy to forget if you live in a Christian bubble like I do, but it's true.

We live in a broken, fallen world, and a lot of it can be traced back to money.

That's not to say that money is bad or that all wealthy people or all successful corporations or industries are evil but just stick with me here. 1 Timothy 6:10 NLT says "For the love of money is the root of all kinds of evil. And some people, craving money, have wandered from the true faith and pierced themselves with many sorrows."

Have you ever heard the expression "the same people who sell the panic sell the pill?" Can you think of other things you could replace panic and pill within this saying? Maybe the same people who sell hysteria sell bubble baths, or the same people who sell insecurities sell beauty products?

Friend, I'm not some crazed naturalist telling you that medicine and bubble bath and beauty products are sinful. I don't believe that they are. What I do believe is that the world we live in sells to us constant reminders that we are lost, broken, or in need. The world tells us we are hopeless. The world tells us we have endless unmet needs. The world tells mamas that they must have lost themselves in motherhood. Turn on the television or open your phone and you are bombarded with advertisements and in those advertisements the world also claims to have the *solutions.* The only way to sell a solution is to shine a light on the problem.

The world sells "lost" because then, they can turn around and sell us a "found" that is profitable. You're temporarily satisfied, until you see another light shining on something else that's wrong with you or your life, and you need to buy something to fix it. We think it's the truth. We really start to believe that we're hopelessly lost, broken, and not good enough. We feel utterly defeated.

But none of that is Biblical. None of that is the life that Jesus has for us.

Jesus says, "I am the light of the world." (John 9:5b). Jesus claims to have a different path out of our lost, broken, not good enough existence. Jesus sees the problems, but He also sees our way out, and He is willing to shine a light on the way out.

Jesus came to save a lost world, and while times have changed, humanity has not. The world is as worldly as it's always been, peddling the concept of lost with a worldly solution. But there's only ever been one solution to our lostness.

It's always been Jesus.

In a world selling lost, we must stand firm in the truths that are in the Word of God. We must seek them out the way Jesus seeks us. We must store up good things in our heart and not listen to the world. Luke 6:45 NLT says "A good person produces good things from the treasury of a good heart, and an evil person produces evil things from the treasury of an evil heart. What you say flows from what is in your heart."

My Momma has this expression she has used on me for as long as I can remember. She says, "trash in, trash out." It really is a Biblical principle. It's what makes it so important that you do exactly what you're doing right now – filling your mind with scripture and Biblical truth, spending time putting on the armor of God (which we'll talk about tomorrow).

The Bible tells us over and over again to stand firm.

If you have on your phone a Bible app that allows you to search for phrases, type in "stand firm" and scroll through all the many verses that appear as a search result.

If you stop and really think about it, how silly is it that we trade in our duty to stand firm for marketing tactics? How silly that we, being rooted in truth and knowing that Jesus came to find us when we were lost, can so easily be led astray simply because someone, somewhere wants to sell us something.

Can you think of anything you've spent money on that was driven by a connection to your identity?

If I buy this outfit, if I start using this makeup, if I get this thing, if I could drive that car...

We were made to love, serve, and glorify God – but we live in a world of aesthetics and serving ourselves through consumerism. Some people look at us and our problems and see dollar signs instead of our souls.

Mama-Sister-Friend, don't give in to a world selling lost. Rest in the arms of a Jesus who came to find you.

Prayer Journal Prompt

Jesus, Thank You for coming to find me when I was at my most lost. I would rather turn to You than any earthly solution. Help me to be aware that the world is out to make me feel lost, but that's not Your truth. I know in my heart that I don't want to look for myself in the world, but in You. Guard me from being tricked by a world selling lost, especially when it has to do with ...

Day 4:
Found Fighting

Ephesians 6:10-13 NKJV

Finally, my brethren, be strong in the Lord and in the power of His might. Put on the whole armor of God, that you may be able to stand against the wiles of the devil. For we do not wrestle against flesh and blood, but against principalities, against powers, against the rulers of the darkness of this age, against spiritual *hosts* of wickedness in the heavenly *places*. Therefore take up the whole armor of God, that you may be able to withstand in the evil day, and having done all, to stand.

My son is almost three and a half at the time of this writing, and he is *obsessed* with good guys and bad guys. When he's playing imaginatively, whether with his dinosaur figurines or with his cars, early on he will distinguish who's the good guy and who's the bad guy.

Now, we've made our home in the middle of the forest, which means our yard is a mere clearing in the woods. When we go outside, all of the bugs, critters, and snakes we come across must be sorted into one of two categories - good guys if they're harmless or bad guys if they bite or sting.

As I sit at my writing desk, the old wooden table that's off the side of our kitchen, my son is in the living room with his daddy. I can hear them talking about which of the toy cars are good guys today, and which ones are bad guys.

All of this good guy and bad guy talk got me thinking about the whole topic as it relates to motherhood. Who's the bad guy to moms?

If I may be perfectly honest, sometimes it feels like my own kid is the bad guy. Can anyone derail plans for a good day as quickly as a headstrong toddler? Sometimes it feels like my husband is the bad guy when he doesn't read my mind or step in to do just the right thing at just the right time in just the right way. But usually, I'm only one deep breath away from remembering that, of course, the people I love most in the world are not *actually* the bad guys. So, who is? Is it me? Some days, it surely feels like that's true, too. On the days where I'm the angry mom, low on patience, or just downright grumpy, I'm sure my family would pinpoint me as the bad guy in the group.

But here's the truth. My sweet child isn't the bad guy. The Bible says children are a gift.

My precious husband isn't the bad guy. The Bible says he deserves my respect.

I'm not the bad guy. The Bible says I'm worth more than rubies.

The Bible says all of us were fearfully and wonderfully made.

Surely, we *can't* be the bad guys if all these things are true.

The Bible tells us very plainly who the bad guy is and how to stand up to him.

The truth is, God didn't bring families together for us to fight and stand against each other. That's not the design He has for our relationships. But look again at our key scriptures for today.

We are commanded to put on the whole armor of God to stand against who?

The devil. The master of confusion. The root of destruction.

The next verses in the Bible, Ephesians 6:14-20, go into detail about what the armor of God includes. And while we may not think of armor as being particularly delicate, beautiful, or feminine, the armor of the Lord applies to everyone because we all go up against the same enemy. It's a shame that so often in our society we pit ourselves against other people. We find ourselves taking sides when it can be just as simple as the way my son views bugs, snakes, and the imaginative games he plays with his toys. There's a good guy and a bad guy. And all mankind is fighting against the same bad guy.

We don't fight against the things we think we fight against. We fight against our one true enemy, the devil. And the only way to stand against him is to stand with God and to clothe ourselves in the armor He's made available to each of us in *every* situation we face.

Our armor is truth, righteousness, peace, faith, salvation, the Holy Spirit, God, and prayer. Our preacher once told my husband to pray through this verse, and I love the idea of walking through the verses and praying on each piece of the armor.

With these things outlined in Ephesians, we have a fighting chance – and we should absolutely be found fighting this battle against darkness. We should be found donning the uniform of gospel ambassadors, and these are the things meant to bring us peace and comfort in the face of all the "bad guys" (and to help us identify who the true bad guy is).

The book of Ephesians ends in the twenty-fourth verse of chapter six, which says in the New King

James Version "Grace be with all those who love our Lord Jesus Christ in sincerity. Amen." That is where I'll leave you today – equipped with your armor, ready to fight, and with abundant grace.

Prayer Journal Prompt

Lord, thank you for this reminder that I'm not the bad guy, and neither are the ones I love so dearly. Even on the most difficult days, hide the truth in my heart that we don't fight against each other but against the enemy, and no-one else. Help me to put on Your full armor, Your full uniform to help me stand against everything meant to cause harm, pain, confusion, and destruction.

Day 5:

 Mamas Know Milk

1 Peter 2:2-3 NLT

Like newborn babies, you must crave pure spiritual milk so that you will grow into a full experience of salvation. Cry out for this nourishment, now that you have had a taste of the Lord's kindness.

I like to think God put this verse in the Bible just for us mamas, because mama … we know milk, don't we? Whether we fed our babies at our breast, fed them from a bottle, or some combination of the two, we know milk. We know what it's like to have a newborn baby crave that milk so badly that it requires round-the-clock attention. We know what it's like to hold a crying infant and know that the only solution is milk. We know what it feels like to step in and save the day with just the right milk.

This is God's desire for us. Sometimes we are crying out, maybe even screaming, because we just need relief. There is a problem and even though we might not realize it at the time, there's only one thing that can fix it.

The solution is like it says in our verse for today – it all comes down to growing in our salvation.

We like to over-complicate things, though, don't we?

When we're feeling lost, when we feel like motherhood and our kids have taken away everything we used to be, when we feel like we just aren't ourselves anymore, when we feel like our entire identity is wrapped up in taking care of other people and their needs – we try to fix it on our own with things like self-care, taking up hobbies, or prioritizing our own needs. There's nothing wrong with those things and they all have their place, but nothing can replace the *milk*.

And we already know this, don't we?

Mama's know milk.

You either know how to keep up your milk supply, or how to supplement, or how to make a bottle for your baby. You know the brand of formula that suits them the best, you know what to eat and what not to eat to best support your milk supply or their sensitive tummies. You know the hunger cues when your baby presents them. You know just what to do when your baby is craving milk, and you know that nothing else could substitute.

Now, imagine yourself as the newborn baby in this verse. The baby who is craving something. The baby who is miserable. The baby who is weak and needy.

God is the solution. God is the answer. God's word is the spiritual milk we all so desperately need. In our key verses today, Peter is trying to explain to us the importance of receiving this nourishment by comparing it to something that stretches across all time and eternity.

I challenge you today to stop looking at your problems as things you need to find solutions for, and to start looking at your problems as cravings for more "milk" of the Word, as the New King James Version puts it.

> *You know just what to do when your baby is craving milk, and you know that nothing else could substitute.*

The things we struggle with, the weaknesses and the shortcomings and the problems we face, are what gives God space in our lives to come in and be the spiritual milk that we need. Paul talks about boasting in his weaknesses because they're the perfect display of Jesus' strengths (2 Corinthians 12:9-10).

Look up that passage and apply it to your life with me. Where I am struggling, He is the solution. Where I am hungry or thirsty, He gives me life. Where I feel lost, He finds me. Where I feel like something is missing, He fills in the gaps.

And if that isn't beautiful enough, God gives us this example of how badly we need Him wrapped up in a verse that *nobody* could understand better than a mother, someone who *knows* milk.

Take today's prayer journaling space today and spend some time being deeply authentic and honest with God, who already knows everything that's inside of you, and talk to Him about what you're craving.

Prayer Journal Prompt

Lord, I just want Your strength to cover my weaknesses. Being totally honest, it sometimes feels like I have the same struggles over and over again. I don't want to keep trying to fix them my way, I know I just need You. I need You like a baby needs milk, especially when it comes to …

Day 6:

Good Things A-Spillin'

Luke 6:45 NKJV

A good man out of the good treasure of his heart brings forth good; and an evil man out of the evil treasure of his heart brings forth evil. For out of the abundance of the heart his mouth speaks.

Look around your house. What are some things overflowing around you right now?

The picture of "overflow" sure is easy for me to visualize. My dishwasher is overflowing. There's probably a laundry hamper overflowing somewhere. My son's crayons are spilling off the kitchen table beside me as I write this devotion. We are overflowing with signs of life in this house. We are overflowing with proof of the things we've stored up in our house – food, clothes, and toys.

What a blessing we take for granted.

But what about our hearts?

Today's key verse is saying that the words we speak, the things we say, come from whatever is in our hearts. This is particularly important to parents because there are impressionable little ears around us. Are you familiar with the little children's song that goes "Oh, be careful little ears what you hear. Oh, be careful little mouths what you speak?" It's a Biblical concept. I try to be so mindful of the words I use in front of my child. Praise the Lord that He cleaned up my potty mouth years ago, but that doesn't mean that there aren't *other* words I don't want my child repeating. I don't want him saying things like stupid,

> *What we put into our hearts and minds is bound to come out, and nobody knows spills like mamas!*

dumb, crap, or shut up. All of those things were off-limits when I was a child, and it's a pattern I want to follow in my own motherhood journey. I would hate to hear such ugly words come out of my innocent child's beautiful little mouth.

I love the illustration of the woman holding her cup of coffee. She bumps into someone and some of her coffee spills out! Do you know *why* the coffee spills? The obvious answer is "her coffee spilled because she bumped into someone." But no, her coffee spilled because coffee was in her cup.

What we put into our hearts and minds is bound to come out, and nobody knows spills like mamas!

Read today's key verses again and let the Holy Spirit lead or possibly convict. Lean into Him. Hear His whispers. What kind of treasure are you storing up in your heart?

I'll tell you that I have recently felt convicted over the things my husband and I watched on tv during date night and the music I listened to in the car. What are these things putting into my heart? I have felt convicted over what happens when I'm angry or stressed or out of patience with my family. How do I behave? What spills out of me when my husband does that thing that just rakes across my last nerve? How do I talk to my child when he has exhausted my last bit of patience for the day?

I believe that sometimes God allows us to find ourselves in situations that show how much we need Him. That goes back to the idea of how God's strength is made perfect in our weakness. Isn't that kind of beautiful?

I was in a Bible study recently and as we studied a passage of scripture and talked as a group about how *good* it was. My friend Jennifer said, "I wish I could put the whole Bible in me." Y'all, how that has stuck with me! I have some scripture memorized, of course not the whole Bible, but wow – how I wish I could just copy and paste and put the whole thing right into my heart.

Maybe *then* I wouldn't be so filthy in sin.

Maybe *then* my heart would be filled with good treasures.

Maybe *then* less ugliness would spill out.

Maybe *then* I would be a better wife and mom.

Maybe *then* I would be a better friend.

Maybe then I would do all the things I think of doing but forget or lack the follow-through to make happen.

I don't know if there is a person alive who could recite the entire Bible, yet the more time we spend in the Word of God, the more material the Holy Spirit has to work with in our hearts and minds. It's the coolest, most supernatural thing when a Bible verse jumps to the forefront of your mind out of seemingly thin air, and you didn't even know that you had it in you.

That is the Holy Spirit at work!

That is when we experience the payoff of working diligently to store up goodness.

I have found that the more time I spend reading my Bible, and allowing the Holy Spirit to convict me, the better off I am. The more time I spend *storing up* goodness, there's less of me and more of God; and that leads to more *goodness* overflowing from me.

We only have room for so much before we overflow. So, what's spilling out? What's in your hypothetical coffee cup when someone bumps into you? What overflows?

Are you able to connect any dots between what you spend time putting in and what comes out? Has the Holy Spirit opened your eyes to some changes you need to make?

Prayer Journal Prompt

God, I realize now the importance of storing up good things so that goodness can overflow from within me. Give me a fierce desire to seek You and to store up Your truths in my heart. Deepen my desire to grow in my relationship with You and knowledge of You. I need your help to …

Day 7:

 God Hears Our Prayers

Psalm 4:3 NLT

You can be sure of this:

The LORD set apart the godly for himself.

The LORD will answer when I call to him.

As my son got older, we started incorporating a bedtime prayer into our routine. It was simple at first, we just thanked God for a few family members by name. As he grew and began talking more, he started asking for more prayer. I had no choice but to oblige him, right?

So, we prayed.

And it seemed like every night our prayers got a little longer. Soon, we were praying for just about every person and animal we'd ever met. Before I knew it, we were thanking God for the various places we went and the different types of construction vehicles we had played with that day.

It was quite humorous with a touch of sweetness, but I eventually saw it for what it was – this was his newest stall tactic to avoid sleep.

So, I came up with a way to try and keep them a little shorter. After we thanked God for our family and friends and beloved pets, all by name, I would close by saying "Thank you, God, for hearing the prayers in our hearts and the prayers that we think. God hears our prayers. Amen."

It took some time for him to adjust, but eventually he accepted that if he had more things he wanted to pray about, he could talk to God in his mind and heart, and that God would hear those prayers, too.

I came across the verse above, Psalm 4:3, and it reminded me of my son and these prayers. My sweet boy and his heart to just talk to God. Even as a young toddler, he knew that God hears his prayers.

And yet, sometimes we forget that it really is just that simple.

Sometimes we forget how nice it is to just be heard by our Heavenly Father.

God cares how we feel.

He cares when we are tired, when we feel worn down, when we feel like we're at the end of our ropes. He cares that we sometimes feel like we are only moms, and nothing else.

He cares because when He created you, He set you apart for himself, and he will hear every prayer you offer up to Him because you are HIS child. He knows every nook and cranny of the heart He put inside your chest and the brain He put inside your head.

God has a solution in His word for everything we come up against.

The Bible is alive. It's the Living Word of God, and if you just open it and seek God with all your heart, He will speak to you. He will comfort you. He will show you the way out of your despair.

He hears you, He cares, and nothing is too small for Him to love you through.

Prayer Journal Prompt

God, I know You love me and care for me, and that You want to hear my prayers. I'm guilty of thinking about some of my problems as being too trivial for You, so right now I want to give You …

Day 8:

After He Answers the Prayer

Psalm 28:6-7 NLT

Praise the LORD!

For he has heard my cry for mercy.

The LORD is my strength and shield.

I trust him with all my heart.

He helps me, and my heart is filled with joy.

I burst out in songs of thanksgiving.

So, what do we do after God answers the prayer we prayed?

God answered a really big prayer of mine – a prayer that I would not have cancer. Come on this journey with me, maybe it has something in common with a journey of your own.

It is Spring 2023 and one of my worst fears has happened – I found a lump in my breast. The fuel behind this fear is a family history of breast cancer. The experience that impacted me the most was when my mom's sister, youthful and healthy and strong, became a cancer patient. My Aunt Lati was diagnosed with breast cancer that ultimately took her life, and while this happened many years ago, I was now about the same age she was when she was diagnosed. I loved my aunt, and we were very close. My heart was completely shattered that she didn't get better this side of eternity, and when I found that lump in my own breast, it felt like the world was crashing down all over again. It just felt too familiar. I attempted to make the earliest available doctor's appointment, calling around to different doctors just trying to find someone who could see me *now*.

I was in a panic. And the panic heightened when the doctor who examined me told me "It's probably nothing, but I'm not going to tell you not to worry." He might as well have looked me straight in the eyes and told me "You probably have cancer, and you should really worry about this and prepare yourself for the worst."

I know that's extreme, but that's how I felt! And when I went for the mammogram and ultrasound of the lump, it was in a building that had unsettling words such as "cancer care center" plastered on what seemed like every available surface and placard. It felt like more than I could handle. It was very much more than what I could handle on my own.

I'll never forget that day. I stood naked, in the world's thinnest "robe" in front of a nurse I had never met before, crying hysterically in response to her simple question – "Any family history of breast cancer?" It was one of the most vulnerable moments of my life, and it happened with a total stranger as my audience.

I leaned on Jesus *so much* during that time. This experience did not last very long in the grand scheme of things, but it felt like a lifetime.

During those three weeks God really worked on me. My patience grew; I was faced with a variety of things that were totally outside my control and all I could do was wait. The results did not come back as quickly as I had hoped, and the medical staff handling the paperwork seemed to be experiencing some sort of breakdown of communication or protocol. Everything that could go wrong went wrong. It was one of those weeks where I spent hours upon hours on the phone talking to the wrong people and waiting on hold. Then my husband got covid, and then our internet went out and then, and then, and then…. It was just a steady stream of something, and I was hanging on by a thread.

I couldn't have gotten through those days without Jesus. I wouldn't have made it without prayer.

And during that time, my prayer tended to be the same one.

Mostly I kept telling God that I was giving the situation to Him - over and over again, because I kept picking it back up so that I could fret and tinker with it and imagine the different scenarios.

Have you ever done that? Given something to God but you just couldn't let it go and so you kept taking it back? It was a real problem for me during this anxious, stressful season.

In the end, God spared me. That's really all there is to say about it. He did not have to protect me from this cancer. I mean, what makes one person more "deserving" than the next? My aunt certainly was not deserving of the cancer that ultimately took her life - a life well lived, I must add. But my tests came back clear, and just three weeks after finding it, the lump was gone. So, now what?

What do I do with this answered prayer, other than finally allow myself to take a good, deep breath of relief? I certainly had a heart full of joy and was perfectly willing to sing my off-key songs of thanksgiving, like in our key verse.

This experience that I went through was so deeply personal. I didn't jump the gun on telling anybody because there was no need for this panic to be widespread. In spite of mentally obsessing over it, I did not particularly want it to be a discussion point. I kept it close. And I think we all do that with the prayers that we pray the hardest.

When our marriage is on the rocks, when we go through a private but serious health scare, when our children are going through horrible difficulties – these aren't the things we talk about. We post smiling pictures of happy faces on social media and the world assumes we live the perfect life because we don't share our deepest struggles. I'm not saying we should air our dirty laundry, but how can we glorify God for carrying us through the storms if we aren't willing to share at least a little about our storms?

God answers prayers; this is a truth our world and our society so desperately needs to hear! But if the only prayers anyone ever hears us pray is asking God to bless the meal before us, and the friends around us; nobody will ever know about the time God pulled you out of despair.

I'm "preaching to the choir", as the old saying goes, because as I'm writing this, I just don't know how to share with the world the way God has answered this prayer of mine - not without letting people in so close to the inner workings of my life, my heart, and my mind. But God is good, and He gave me an example of His goodness that I can share with others! Am I going to do it? I will. I'm a writer, you know? I'll write the story, and I'll share it somehow. But I pose the same question to you. What do we do after God answers our prayers?

Some of us are very private while some of us tend to be more of an open book, but our struggles and God's goodness are the stories we need to share. Someone needs to hear *your* story.

I don't believe that we are automatically required to tell everybody everything about our personal lives, or to share deeply personal experiences on social media simply

I'm not saying we should air our dirty laundry, but how can we glorify God for carrying us through the storms if we aren't willing to share at least a little about our storms?

because God answered a prayer. But what do we do with it?

There is no one-size-fits-all answer here, but I'll leave you with a verse to go look up on your own.

James 4:17

If you feel like you have a story to tell and God is nudging you towards sharing it (either publicly or with just one person), think about this verse and follow where God leads.

Prayer. Journal. Prompt.

Lord, I just want to take a moment and praise You and to thank you for answering my prayers in the perfect way that only You can. You aren't boxed in by my limited way of thinking. You are omnipotent, Your ways are better than my ways, and You answered my prayers beyond my wildest dreams and imaginations. So, now Lord, I want You to tell me what to do with them. Who needs to hear about Your goodness to me? Show me …

Day 9:

 Accepting a Lot

Ecclesiastes 5:18-20 NLT

Even so, I have noticed one thing, at least, that is good. It is good for people to eat, drink, and enjoy their work under the sun during the short life God has given them, and to accept their lot in life. And it is a good thing to receive wealth from God and the good health to enjoy it. To enjoy your work and accept your lot in life – this is indeed a gift from God. God keeps such people so busy enjoying life that they take no time to brood over the past.

My husband and I had been married for two years when we got the shock of our lives – I was pregnant. And neither of us wanted children. I was not sure about many things in life, but I was certain that I did not want to be a mother. There were so many selfish thoughts in my heart. All our plans were gone. Not only that, but we were also being catapulted in the opposite direction of every single life plan we had on our books. It seemed like too much. I didn't go to work for days, opting instead to lay in bed and wallow in my sorrows. Finally, my boss called me and told me to pull myself together and come back to work. She knew

I was heartbroken, and she truly was understanding and compassionate towards me while also being the voice of reason. She told me exactly what I needed to hear! It was time to accept my circumstances and just enjoy God's blessings.

Can you relate to any part of this story?

I share it with you to say this:

God has so much encouragement for us in His word, truly there is something for every circumstance. Thinking on your own life, read our key verse for today again as we set up house here and unpack for a while.

If we broke this passage of scripture down into a checklist, it'd look like this:

- ❋ **Enjoy your work.**
- ❋ **Remember life is short.**
- ❋ **Accept your lot in life.**
- ❋ **Receive wealth from God.**
- ❋ **Acknowledge good health.**
- ❋ **Enjoy & accept.**
- ❋ **Do all of this, and you'll be busy – not brooding.**

Maybe that seems oversimplified, especially in cases where accepting our lot in life is sometimes asking us to accept … well … a lot. Is this really life?

What about the discontented newborn who just won't sleep? Or the teething infant? Sometimes those cries permeate us to the core. Don't overlook the strong-willed and defiant toddler who has a full daily itinerary of testing boundaries and pulling dangerous stunts. Then there's the sass and constant questioning of a young child. We aren't even talking about the preteen and teenage years – hard questions, puberty, first crushes and heartbreaks, big issues of trust and independence. All of that tucked in nice and cozy beside everything else that falls under the motherhood umbrella like cleaning, cooking, and keeping up with everybody's everything. You know better than anyone, life is busy, and some days are just hard. Yep, that's a lot to accept alright.

Perhaps this passage from Ecclesiastes is the perfect helper for a busy, sometimes frazzled, mama. Let's go through it, item by item.

✳ Enjoy your work.

Insert grumbles from mamas everywhere, right? Nobody enjoys *everything,* do they? It feels like the chores are never-ending sometimes and like we will never get to the top of Mount Everest's cousin, Mount Laundry. As mothers, our tasks are often thankless. But the Bible says it is good to enjoy our work! How? We can work as if we are working for God, because Mama-Sister-Friend, we *are*. (Colossians 3:23-24.)

❋ Remember life is short.

We've all heard the cliche advice passed down from generation to generation, one mother to another – the days are long, but the years are short. Who knew it was Biblical?! Still, we've heard that before, and it isn't particularly encouraging when we're trapped in seasons that seem to go on forever. However, life *is* short, and we know this. We see that our kids are growing up apparently in between our own blinks. We see evidence of the passage of time. So, I rather like that this reminder is tucked into the holy pages of God's word. It is a reminder that we humans have proven we need, and we need it often. Nothing lasts forever.

❋ Accept your lot in life.

All of us have such different lives, but yet, they can have so much in common! It's amazing. I wholeheartedly believe that what we look for in this life, we will find.

Imagine you and I just sat down for a nice warm cup of coffee in a cozy little café. It's our first time meeting, but we've already decided that we don't have anything in common. So, we sit there in silence, picking the other apart in our brains and using what we see to confirm our opinions. But what if we had just accepted each other, the differences and all, and found some common ground? We could be friends, I bet. After all, we *are* of the same species, and we at least have motherhood in common. We could talk about that. We could talk about our walks of faith. We could talk about coffee! We could find friendship if we resolved to leave that meeting with a new friend because what we look for, we find. The same goes for contentment, my friend. If we look at our lives and only take inventory of the things that are wrong, we will breed further discontentedness. This passage from Ecclesiastes urges us *twice* to accept our lot in life. What does acceptance look like in motherhood? We have to let go of anger, bitterness, and resentment. We cannot let comparison steal our joy. We take inventory of our blessings, and all that God has blessed us with, and not focus on what we wish we had or on what someone else has that may appear better. Acceptance sounds a lot like peace and joy, doesn't it? More than that, it sounds like freedom.

❋ Receive wealth from God.

Once we have accepted our lot in life, and chosen to focus on our blessings, we can truly start to receive our wealth from God. Allow me to explain.

Wealth does not come *only* in the form of money, though, does it? King Solomon, the writer of Ecclesiastes, was rich. Not only that, but he was one of the wealthiest people named in the Bible. I cannot personally relate to his wealth of gold and treasures ... but now that I've thought about it, I *am* a wealthy woman. I can count my riches in love, security, family, warmth, and even the air in my lungs. In terms of motherhood, becoming a mother is like marrying into a royal family where the riches keep unfolding year after year. (Sure, with those riches comes great responsibility, but that is always the case with riches, is it not?)

What makes *you* wealthy in a way that is not measured with dollar signs?

It's almost as if accepting our lot in life opened our hearts up to appreciating all that God has given us. So, we receive this wealth, whatever it may include, from God and with our good health, we enjoy it.

❊ Acknowledge our good health.

What about the mothers who do not have good health? In our world, we see chronic diseases and disorders, cancer, debilitating depression or anxiety, amongst other ailments. Just as everyone is not given the same wealth, we are not all given the same health. We *can*, however, take in God's goodness wherever it is, and regardless of how it looks in comparison to someone else's. I watched my aunt battle breast cancer for years. She had, at one point, two young children. As a cancer patient herself, she buried her infant. But still, she outwardly practiced gratitude. Her legacy outlives her, and that legacy is that she did everything she could to make the most of the little scraps of health she could find. She was a silver-lining-finder if there ever was one, and she will forever inspire me. I hope I can pass that inspiration on to you, too. There are no guarantees in this life, but we can make the most of what we have. I believe that is what King Solomon, and God, are trying to tell us in these verses.

Perhaps our wealth and health have more to do with perspective and gratitude than it does with dollar signs and bank accounts or doctor appointments and medications or even lack thereof.

❋ Enjoy and accept.

We are called, once again, as King Solomon repeats his urgings that we enjoy and accept. Not always easy and sometimes accepting our lot in life is accepting a lot, but we can do that with God's help. We can do anything with God's help, can't we? And when we enjoy and accept, these verses end with a promise.

❋ Do all of this, and you'll be busy not brooding.

The promise is this: We will be *busy* enjoying God's gift of life. This verse reminds us that there is more value in reflecting on God and the inner joy He provides us today, the blessings He has given us today, than on days gone by. I get it, perhaps better than most, how tempting it can be to remember the past. My history is complicated – it is one that is filled with adventure and passion, of which I have countless fond memories, but I was also living a sinful life, and my heart was hardened against God. Looking back and daydreaming isn't always something that serves us well.

God is telling us that we can follow King Solomon's checklist, and it will help us be busy enjoying our blessings. How wonderful does that sound?! Life is already busy, crazy busy. Motherhood is a wild ride, no denying it and no changing it. What *can* change? We can change. We can accept our lot, we can accept a lot with God's help, and we can just enjoy this season the best we can. We can enjoy the ride. Like how a rollercoaster can be thrilling, it can also be dreadful and terrifying and unpredictable at moments. One thing is for certain, though. The end will come, sometimes abruptly, and we'll be left breathless and wondering how something can begin and pass and end so suddenly.

Sometimes we need someone to just tell us to pull ourselves together. This verse can do that for us, but in the most loving way. It's that reminder than no matter what God has put in our lives, we can accept it and enjoy His gifts, and it really can be as simple as accepting our lot, even when it's a lot.

Prayer Journal Prompt

Lord, Sometimes I feel like life is just hard, that it's all too much sometimes. I know I need to accept my lot in life, enjoy my work, and live abundantly in the blessings You have poured out over me. Thank You, God, for this life. Help me to accept it for all that it is and all that it isn't. Deposit your

joy in my heart so that I can be busy enjoying
this life. Help me accept ...

Day 10:

 The Found Mama

John 7:37 NLT

On the last day, the climax of the festival, Jesus stood and shouted to the crowds, "Anyone who is thirsty may come to me!"

John 8:12 NLT

Jesus spoke to the people once more and said, "I am the light of the world. If you follow me, you won't have to walk in darkness, because you will have the light that leads to life."

What does it mean to be a "Found Mama?" Where did that phrase come from? What does it really mean and who is it talking about?

The Found Mama is the opposite of the mama who lost herself in motherhood. My heart breaks when I see mothers on social media sharing posts that include those words. As Christians, we cannot be lost. It really is as simple as that.

In our two key verses today, Jesus is comparing Himself to basic needs and we are going to connect this to our identities and what it means to be Found in Jesus.

Back when Jesus walked the earth, light and water would have been considered two of the most basic needs. Without electricity, everything would have been very different. I imagine most people went to sleep when the sky darkened after dusk. Candles and lanterns would have been limited resources for most people. As for water, life would have revolved around sources of water. There were limited beverage options, and no homes would have running water for quite some time. Laundry, bathing, and cooking needs would all require water that required effort. Needing water and light would have been top priorities.

Have you ever lost power and been without light? Have you ever been without water? It can be hard to function!

Growing up in coastal South Carolina, hurricanes are a threat to us every season. I used to love losing power and having to rough it for a few days when I was a child. My mom would heat up canned goods on the grill. We would light candles and play board games.

As a mama to two young kids myself now, losing power is not my favorite thing because it disrupts our routines. This is when I am most reminded that light and water are two pretty important things. Even when I take them for granted, they're still two of the most basic needs.

What does this have to with finding our identity in Jesus? When we are grappling with matters of who we are and what our identities are rooted in, Jesus is just as basic of a need as water and light.

Just like with light and water, there are no substitutes, and there is no substitute for Jesus. The human body was designed to require water; the human eye cannot see in true darkness. In order to function, we must have water. In order to function, we must have light. In order to function, we must have Jesus.

Who we are has to be woven together with who Jesus says we are. We hear this verse at weddings, but Ecclesiastes 4:12 comes to mind. The NLT reads, "A person standing alone can be attacked and defeated, but two can stand back-to-back and conquer. Three are even better, for a triple-braided cord is not easily broken." Can we apply this to who we are in Jesus? Can we apply this to our identity? What do you think the three strands would be?

At first, I think of the Trinity and the way God holds us together so completely by being the Father who loves, the Savior who sacrificed, and the Holy Spirit who guides. If every other thing about us, if every other part of our identity, was being held together by *that* three-braided strand, there would never be any doubt that we are found in Jesus, not lost in motherhood.

We talked before about how losing ourselves in motherhood is a lie from the enemy meant to destroy, but destruction can take on different forms. Perhaps destruction can even come in the form of a distraction. Dare to consider, feeling like we lost ourselves means we aren't focusing on who God says we are and what He says is true. Our attention has shifted, and our eyes are no longer on God, but on ourselves.

I know it is hard being a mama. You are safe here. I have hard days, too, just like all moms. Not a single word of this book is being written by a perfect mother who has it all figured out. I'm right here in the trenches with you, Mama-Sister-Friend. Through my own struggles, this is what I've learned:

- It doesn't matter what else you find. Until you find Jesus, you will always be searching.

- Without living water, we will always be thirsty.

- Without the light of the world, every place will be dark.

- Without Jesus, we will always feel like something is missing and everything we try will, eventually, leave us lost.

This is what it's all about. Finding Jesus. Running to Him when we are thirsty. Trusting Him to be the light in the darkness. Because when we find Him, we find ourselves. When we truly find Him, we realize how little all the other things matter.

I promise that I am not trying to imply that you don't know Jesus. I mean something else entirely, actually. Can I tell you one more story?

I was pregnant with my first born and sitting in Sunday school one morning. We go to a small church, and our classes are intimately small and cozy, warm and honest. It's nice. But the only reason I went to Sunday school at that time, truthfully, is because I knew if I didn't, my mom would be disappointed in my husband and me. Do you believe in divine appointments? I sure do, because this one Sunday changed my life. This one particular morning, the discussion question was posed: Who is the strongest Christian you know? Everyone goes around the room, answering, and most of us had the same answer. It was our parents. *That* was when it hit me: One day, my little baby growing in my womb could be asked that same question. I wanted him to be able to say it was his parents, too. With that realization came another - I was going to have to make some changes if I wanted to be that for my children. Easier said than done, sure, that was when Jesus really started coming alive to me. That was when a real relationship with Him began to unfold as I drew nearer to Him with my whole heart and experienced Him reciprocating.

That is my hope for you, too. I hope that Jesus feels alive for you and that there is a relationship.

> *When we find Him, we find ourselves. When we truly find Him, we realize how little all the other things matter.*

That does not come simply through salvation. We have to make an effort. He found us when He saved us, but that cannot be the end. We have to stick with Him!

That is what being a Found Mama truly means.

As a Found Mama, you can look at your life and see the way God has always had a plan.

You'll begin realizing that your life is so much more than finding yourself – it's about losing your selfishness and finding more of Jesus.

If you have felt like you lost yourself in motherhood but it's leading you to find yourself in Jesus, then thinking yourself lost was the best thing that ever happened to you.

The last thing this world needs is the lost version of me and you.

What you and I need, and what this world needs - is more of Jesus, and the certainty and the joy He gives. That needs to be the most prominent thing about us!

Prayer Journal Prompt ·

Jesus, I want to depend on You for every basic need. I want You to be my water and my light. I want my identity to be so completely wrapped up in You that …

Day 11:

 Found in Jesus

Proverbs 3:5-6 NLT

Trust in the Lord with all your heart; do not depend on your own understanding. Seek his will in all you do, and he will show you which path to take.

At this point, you've probably caught on to the fact that we are going to talk a lot about the concepts of being lost and being found. When everything is boiled down, that's really all there is. Lost or found, good or evil. Let's dive in on what it means to be found in Jesus.

In short, it means that the most important part of our identity is that we are children of the King. And specifically, as moms, it means that you've found the truth that God has placed the important assignment of motherhood on your head, and you are accepting what that involves from a Biblical perspective. You don't feel like you're lost in motherhood because you've found the truth. This is the life Jesus wants for you. This is the story He chose to plant you in, and are you blooming? You've resolved to lean on the Bible for understanding, not the world. You've decided to draw your strength from God instead of whatever trendy buzzword the world is pushing on you at any given moment – like self-care, manifestations, treating yourself, etc.

Jesus says in John 10:10 NLT, "The thief's purpose is to steal and kill and destroy. My purpose is to give them a rich and satisfying life."

He called the devil a thief! That's what he does, he takes things away from us under the pretense that he can offer us something better than anyone else. Imagine a man in a trench coat selling beautiful, but broken watches. The devil is a thief, a con artist, and a corrupt businessman. What's his business? He is in the business of souls, and he knows that God is his competition. I once heard that the devil has no new tactics, and I found so much comfort in that idea that I wanted to share it with you. He is doing the same things he has always done – stealing, killing, destroying. He is the master of confusion and Jesus, ah, well Jesus is the opposite in every way. He does not steal things from us, He gives. He does not kill, but He gives life to even dry bones. He does not destroy, He restores.

We must know who we are. We must know who Jesus says we are. If we don't, if there is even an ounce of confusion about who we are in Christ, how will we ever hope to establish in our children's hearts who Jesus says they are? How can we if we aren't sure about who *we* are in Jesus? We must get our groundwork right and we can only do that by walking more and more closely to the Lord. We will find our identities in God when we are looking for our identities with God.

James 4:8 NLT says, "Come close to God, and God will come close to you. Wash your hands, you sinners; purify your hearts, for your loyalty is divided between God and the world."

It never feels good to be called a sinner, but it is true, we are all sinners. If you go through this verse piece by piece, it can be a blueprint to be found in Jesus. The first step is to make an intentional effort to be in the presence of God. We cannot be found in Jesus if we aren't *with* Jesus. Then, the instruction to wash our hands is interesting because we know that when we get saved, Jesus washes us clean. So why the instruction to wash our hands? Perhaps because we tend to pick up old habits or hold onto things we should let go. Finally, we're told to turn away from worldly things. The Message translates this same verse to say, "So let God work his will in you. Yell a loud no to the Devil and watch him make himself scarce. Say a quiet yes to God and he'll be there in no time. Quit dabbling in sin. Purify your inner life. Quit playing the field. Hit bottom and cry your eyes out. The fun and games are over. Get serious, really serious. Get down on your knees before the Master; it's the only way you'll get on your feet." That sure sounds like being found in Jesus, doesn't it?

Our key verses today, from Proverbs 3:5-6 gives us further instruction as to *how* to be found in Jesus, *how* to make sure we are on His path. We cannot rely on ourselves to figure this out because we are sinful. We will not find it in the world, because the world is ugly and broken. It's not something we can understand on our own – it's something we absolutely must find in Jesus. Drawing near to Him and reading our Bibles is *how* we stop depending on our own understandings and start seeking God's will and God's path for our lives and who it is He wants us to become. Our identity does not come from our titles, relationships, jobs, parenting styles, or anything else. Our identity comes from Jesus. Period. The only thing required of us is surrender it all to Him. And when we do?

Psalm 73:28 NLT says, "But as for me, how good it is to be near God! I have made the Sovereign LORD my shelter, and I will tell everyone about the wonderful things you do."

When we look for God, we will find Him. And when we are with Him, we will see Him working all around us. It will be *so good* that we will not be able to stop talking about His goodness! Isn't that exciting?!

Right now, my son is sitting beside me looking for dinosaur eggs in his oatmeal and finding them because he is looking in the right place – in his bowl of dinosaur egg oatmeal! If we're looking for evil, we will find evil. If we're looking for God, we will find Him. If we are looking for evidence of God's goodness, we will find evidence. If we are looking for things to be grateful for, we will experience gratitude. If we are looking for things to complain about, we will experience despair. If we are looking for contentment, we will find peace. If we believe the world when it tells us that we have lost ourselves in motherhood, and we start looking for evidence of this in our own lives, we will find it. However, if we read the Bible, searching for scripture and truths that we can apply to motherhood and our identities, we will find them, too! We will find them in abundance.

If we are looking for ourselves in Jesus, we will find ourselves there. We will find who He says we are. This is what it means to be found in Jesus instead of being lost in motherhood.

Prayer Journal Prompt

Lord, I am guilty of giving in to what the world says and not leaning fully on what You say. I want to be the woman You say I am. I want to find my identity in You, Jesus.

I want to pray a prayer of protection around myself and my family right now. In Jesus name, the thief is not welcome here. The devil cannot have...

_____

_____

_____

_____

_____

_____

_____

_____

_____

Forgive me for giving into the worldly idea that I can lose who I am. I know You made me, You put me here with a purpose, and You created me to glorify and worship You. Guide me into finding out who You say I am. Help me to...

Day 12:

 Choosing Sin

Proverbs 27:12 NLT

A prudent person foresees danger and takes precautions. The simpleton goes blindly on and suffers the consequences.

Have you ever deliberately and knowingly chosen sin over God?

I lived out several years of my life where I chose my sins over God, too many years if I'm being perfectly honest. When I say I chose my sin, I *really* chose it. I knew God. I knew His goodness. After having grown up in a Christian home and accepting Jesus into my heart I grew up and walked away and lived a *hard* life. But I did repent, I got back on track, I came home to Jesus' arms, and He made it all right. And when I say *it,* I mean my heart, my soul, my life became *all right.*

Once again, I could call myself a Christian with a clear conscious.

During this time, I really did love the Lord, and I tried to serve Him to the best of my ability. I don't quite know how to explain what happened next, but things fell apart. My life fell apart. *Again.* I was angry at God for the way some of my life plans worked out because I felt I had done everything "right" this time and yet, I was still left in a mess with a broken heart.

Maybe you've felt like this before, as if you were living through a punishment you did not deserve. When I felt that way, I made the ugly choice to walk away from living an obedient life that honored God. I distanced myself from God in every possible way, and either my ears were closed to the Holy Spirit or He had left me alone as a lost cause. Both of those options send a chill down my spine to this day. But it's the truth, I chose sin over God, knowing full and well what I was going back to and what I was leaving behind. I went running back to things God had already rescued me from.

By the time I got married to my husband, Alan, I knew that I wanted to "do better," but that was just kind of a vague goal, and it was more cartilage than bone. But at some point, God will confront us with the choice. Will we choose a relationship with God *over* choosing sin? It can't be both.

There is no union between sin and God. We touched on this yesterday when we looked at James 4:8 and talked about divided loyalty.

For me, it was easy to leave behind the sinful things when I knew that my choices were dangerous. Some would say that's overly dramatic or theatrical, but honestly, it's simpleminded to think of the things that separate us from God as anything other than dangerous. Even if they are little things, if they keep us from God, then they're dangerous. Period. And no amount of justification will change that. That's what our key verse is telling us today! We can see sin for what it is, or we can suffer the consequences. It is that simple.

When God made us mothers, He gave us the responsibility of creating a refuge for our children. It is our duty to see danger and take precautions on behalf of our children because they cannot do it for themselves. We cannot turn a blind eye to the evils of this world.

That can mean leaving a lot of stuff behind. What does that mean to you?

Consider this.

You're walking through the woods, taking a little scenic hike through nature, when suddenly you realize a snake, a venomous snake, has wrapped itself around your shoe and is starting to work its way up your leg.

What do you do?

    A. Keep it as a pet
    B. Say, "Hey little friend" and gently take him off and set him on the ground right beside you
    C. See the snake wrapped around your shoe and ignore it
    D. Grab hold of it, fling it off and throw it as far as you can

Now consider this.

Satan came in the form of a serpent.

It's dangerous to keep our sins as pets; it's even dangerous to take our sins off but keep them close. The Bible says to throw them off because they can so easily tangle us right back up.

Hebrews 12:1 NIV says "Therefore, since we are surrounded by such a great cloud of witnesses, let us throw off everything that hinders and the sin that so easily entangles. And let us run with perseverance the race marked out for us."

Throw it off.

Don't set it down gently. Don't put it up on a shelf where you can see it. Don't hide it in the back of the closet. Throw. It. Off.

Throw it off like the dangerous thing that it is.

This example from my own life won't apply to everyone. When I feel the most "lost" is when I look back at my old life and compare the fun of that life to the responsibility of this life. I can't ignore the fact that my old life was also very riddled with ugly, dark, sin. Maybe I feel lost in motherhood sometimes, but a lot of those things needed to get lost, honestly. Losing that version of myself has been, in many ways, a blessing and a complete necessity. If you can relate to my story, I challenge you to adjust your way of thinking about your past in a rosy, romanticized glow and to start looking at it for what it is – a life full of dangerous sin that had to be thrown off in order to be a good mom.

> *When God made us mothers, He gave us the responsibility of creating a refuge for our children. It is our duty to see danger and take precautions on behalf of our children because they cannot do it for themselves. We cannot turn a blind eye to the evils of this world.*

If you can relate to my story, this first prayer journal prompt is yours.

If you do not relate to my story, then consider what sins you're keeping around as a pet and what you need to throw off like the dangerous thing it is. That could be anything from gossiping to secret habits to the entertainment you consume – only you know what God is speaking into your heart. The second prayer journal prompt is yours.

Prayer Journal Prompt

Thank You, God, for rescuing me from my chosen sin and forgive me for ever looking back on them fondly. Help me to view my life today as a refuge. Help me to wisely see the danger of anything that keeps me away from You, so that I don't keep going and cause suffering for myself and my family later. It's hard for me to....

Prayer Journal Prompt

Thank you, God, for speaking to my heart about the sin in my life that keeps me from walking closer to You. Show me how to throw it off so that I can take refuge in You and raise my children in a way that most honors You. I know I've been holding onto ...

Day 13:

 Having It All Together

Philippians 3:12-14 MSG

I'm not saying that I have this all together, that I have it made. But I am well on my way, reaching out for Christ, who has so wonderfully reached out for me. Friends, don't get me wrong: By no means do I count myself an expert in all of this, but I've got my eye on the goal, where God is beckoning us onward – to Jesus. I'm off and running, and I'm not turning back.

Writing this book at the ripe age of 33 has been a calling God placed on my heart as long ago as the fourth grade; when I declared that I was going to be a writer and an author. That's where it started on my end, at least. Ever since, I've gone through the ebb and flow of writing this or that, or not writing at all and trying to do anything else because writing is "weird" and vulnerable. And so finally, here we are. I'm so happy you're here with me and I genuinely hope and pray that you are getting something out of this book that I have poured so much heart, soul, and prayer into over hours and hours of work and studying and writing.

My number one priority here, and my first hope, is that this book points you to Jesus in a new way. In a way that at the end of this book, your relationship with Jesus has grown, and expanded, and bled into more areas of your life – because that's what blood does, it spreads, and it covers. It makes a big mess, it wrecks everything. I hope that the blood of Jesus has done that to your heart and your life. We all have to be continually pointed to Jesus, we all have to continuously let the blood of Jesus wash over us. It's a lifelong journey, a lifelong need. I hope that, even if just for a little while, that this book fills that need in your life.

A secondary goal of mine is to share enough of me with you that you feel a little more normal, and a little less alone in your own motherhood journey. It's amazing to me how alone we can feel in our own homes, in our roles as moms, and even at times feeling alone in the world – but we are not alone. We are *never* alone. By sharing the more personal parts of my life with you, I hope that someone, somewhere will feel less alone, even if just for a moment.

One of the best parts about having mom friends is that you have someone in your life who can put your worries at ease and say things like "I feel that way sometimes, too." or "My kid does the exact same thing!" It's also one of the more beautiful parts of social media – connection, solidarity, finding mom friends from all over the world!

Not only is God with us, but the Bible also tells us in Ecclesiastes 1:9 NKJV that "there is nothing new under the sun." So even when we feel totally alone, it's important to call that feeling out as the lie from the enemy that it truly is, because we aren't alone, and we are not the first person to experience whatever it is that we are living. That lie is an attempt to divide and conquer us. Jesus is quoted as saying these words in Matthew 18:20, "For where two or three come together in my name, there am I with them." This can mean for moms that, together, we can meet before Jesus in our motherhood struggles, and hardships, and trials, and even triumphs - and Jesus will show up and be right there with us in the midst of, well, anything.

Today, let's chat about this one particular lie that sometimes sneaks in and disguises itself as truth, and that's the lie that we are supposed to have it all together. And so many of us don't feel that way about our lives *at all*. It's hard when so much of social media is drenched with the image of perfection and togetherness (Ah, the pitfall of the internet!). We get caught up in comparing all of the ways we just aren't like what we see on the internet. I'm guilty of these things, too, even when it comes to writing this book. The book that I *know* the Lord has placed a calling on my life to write. It's so hard sometimes to not compare!

This is an excerpt from my personal, private prayer journal dated May 14, 2022.

 "Lord, I'm so excited about the book You've given me to write. And I want to keep doing all of the work on social media as well, but I feel like it isn't really resonating with people as much as I had hoped, so that makes me feel like I'm doing something wrong. I guess this is one thing that makes social media so dangerous — I've been so sure that this is <u>Your</u> plan for me, fully convinced that this is Your path for me — but yet if it's not performing well on Instagram, I begin to doubt. Doubt myself, doubt my calling, doubt my abilities, doubt if You're really here on this path or if I've got it all wrong. And I know that's not fueled by feelings from You — it's that social media comparison."

Sometimes, we can be right where we are supposed to be, but what we see on social media can make us feel inferior. Isn't it horrible that we give the internet that much power over our *feelings*? How can the internet fuel some fires while simultaneously putting out others? Especially considering that nobody really, truly has it *all* together.

Sometimes these types of feelings and comparing our lives to what we see on social media can make us feel like we've lost ourselves in motherhood. Either we see other people who have their lives more together than we do, or we compare our lives now to the way things used to be before children. Before chaos, once upon a time, long ago.

So, my friend, today I just want to encourage you, and remind you, you're really not supposed to have it all together. What you see on social media is often fake. Social media rarely paints a full picture and is often just a zoomed in shot of the prettiest parts of life. Nobody has it all together. And here's the very best part, if we *did* have it all together, we wouldn't need Jesus.

I'm truly obsessed with the way the Message translated the verses from Philippians I've put at the top of today's devotional. Having it all together is not important. Being an expert doesn't matter. Perfection is irrelevant.

The NLT version of this same scripture, Philippians 3:12-14, reads:

"I don't mean to say that I have already achieved these things or that I have already reached perfection. But I press on to possess that perfection for which Christ Jesus first possessed me. No, dear brothers and sisters, I have not achieved it, but I focus on this one thing: Forgetting the past and looking forward to what lies ahead, I press on to reach the end of the race and receive the heavenly prize for which God, through Christ Jesus, is calling us."

There is something so much more important than having it all together – and that's forgetting the past and leaning into the future that Jesus has for us.

It's Jesus, y'all! The answer is always Jesus!

We don't have to have it all together – but we have to have Jesus.

God designed all of us as humans to need Him. Take comfort in the fact that your imperfections and struggles and hardships, and all the things in your life that make you feel like a failure, are the very things that keep you going back to God. Keep working through them, keeping working on yourself with God, keep taking your sins and your shortcomings to Him in prayer - and He will help you. But just know that you will never reach perfection. And that's okay. You weren't created to reach perfection in this life.

You were created to worship and glorify God, you were created to be a mother, you were created to be an imperfect person serving a perfect Savior and pointing others to Him in a way that only you can.

Prayer Journal Prompt

Jesus, I need you. Too many times, I rely on myself to pull everything together when I should be leaning on you. Having You is the most important thing in the world, and I hate that sometimes I lose sight of that. I realize that nobody has it all together, and that is not what You ask of me. I feel inferior and sometimes insecure when I compare my life to …

Day 14:

Authentic Motherhood

Ecclesiastes 1:9 NLT

History merely repeats itself. It has all been done before. Nothing under the sun is truly new.

One thing I believe in wholeheartedly is that if there is a problem, Jesus is the solution. If we feel lost in motherhood, turning to Jesus will help us feel found. If we feel burdened, Jesus will carry the weight. If we feel burnt out, good news, Jesus is the light of the world! If we feel alone, we have a friend in Jesus. I really, truly believe these things.

Apart from Jesus being the ultimate solution, there is one little tool I have in my toolbelt that helps me when motherhood feels particularly interactive. Whether it's a basic need like food, clothing, bathing or if it's something more trivial like needing to be entertained, or someone needing an audience while they provide the entertainment nobody asked for ... there's just very little time to sit and be *me.* Honestly, sometimes it makes me wish momentarily that things were different. What makes you feel that way?

One thing that helps me though those moments is just a simple reminder to myself to be authentic. I do not have to pretend that those moments do not happen, I just have to work through those moments in a way that honors God.

This is how I check in with myself in those moments:

What am I feeling right now? *Feel it and pray about it.*

What do I wish I was doing right now? *Do it – and bring the kids along.*

How do I wish this moment was different? *Make it different.*

I know, I know. That sounds overly simple, but it can be just that simple! It can be as simple as giving yourself permission to feel how you feel. Let your feelings rush across you like waves, give the things to Jesus that you need to give away. Feel them and then let them go. Change what you can and surrender what you need to surrender.

Do the things that you love but make them a family activity! It's okay if it looks a little different with kids around, and it's okay if it takes a little practice. You won't regret incorporating your passions into the way you parent. Do you like to paint? Paint with your kids! Do you like to read? Set up a cozy reading nook and work on practicing quiet reading time. Do you like gardening? Garden with your kids – there are very inexpensive child gardening supplies for beginners or teach them how to safely use your tools and work alongside them. (OR, ya know, people probably used to garden with their hands or spoons or just whatever they had available!) Let our verse from today ring true in your life and just find a way to make the things that are important to you *happen.* I think sometimes we're guilty of considering ourselves and our circumstances to be unicorns, but here in our key verse today the Bible says that "it has all been done before."

There's nothing about your situation that hasn't happened to someone else before.

You are not the first mom to feel the way you feel. You are not the first painter afraid to bring out art supplies around the kids or the first gardener fearful of what could go wrong with a child and sharp gardening tools. You aren't the first! We can even look back at history and find examples of people who thought they were the first, but they weren't (looking at you, Christopher Columbus). Let that be a comfort to you, let it inspire you to *just do the thing.*

I'm going to give you a fill-in-the-blank. I want you to think about filling this blank in with some sort of life-giving hobby or activity. What would feel most authentic to you and make you feel most like yourself?

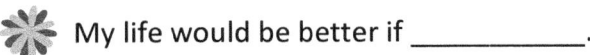 My life would be better if _____.

Now, make it happen with your kids. Find a way to do it with them. It might look different than it did without children in the picture. Actually, I can guarantee it will look different. Adjust your expectations, prepare your heart to approach a new thing with patience, be authentic and honest about the way you feel – and live out an authentic motherhood lifestyle and journey that feels like the real you. As you are doing this activity with your children, talk to them about how this can honor God or how we can use our talents to serve God or point others to Him.

Having kids doesn't mean watching cartoons and singing nursery rhymes 24/7. Make this journey your own. Get creative, think outside the box, and get busy living authentically as a mom.

Your homework for today is to make a plan of how you are going to execute this activity so that it does not get lost in the shuffle of life. Can you make it happen today? Do you need to work on a plan for when you can make it happen? You've got this, Mama.

Remember, the way you feel is not unique to you. After all, "There is nothing new under the sun." So, while the way you feel is not unique, the way you live it out certainly is, especially as a Believer! We don't all have to be the same mom. You can be our own person - a unique, authentic mom and still be a good mom, and odds are, you won't even be the first one to give it a shot.

Prayer Journal Prompt ·

Lord, show me how to be a mom that is authentic and honoring of you and the person you made me to be. Sometimes I get caught up in thinking my situation is so unique that nobody could understand or find a solution to my problems. Thank You for reminding me that there is nothing new under the sun, and that there is always a solution when I take my problems to You. I really think I would enjoy motherhood more if I could find a way to do what I love. Help me prioritize and organize a way to ...

Day 15:

 Realistic Expectations

John 14:26-27 NLT

But when the Father sends the Advocate as my representative – that is, the Holy Spirit – he will teach you everything and will remind you of everything I have told you. I am leaving you with a gift – peace of mind and heart. And the peace I give is a gift the world cannot give. So don't be troubled or afraid.

Part of the trick to being authentic is knowing what you want and pinpointing your expectations.

You cannot live your most authentic life if you don't know what the goal is. However, we also have to check in on whether or not our goals are realistic while checking our hearts and desires against the Bible.

I was visiting with a friend once and she was rehashing her early days of motherhood. Let's call her Rebekah. Rebekah shared with me what a struggle it was for her in the beginning as a mother, but that was no surprise. We've all been there! I nodded in agreement because I certainly had felt that struggle myself. What she said next surprised me!

She took full responsibility for her struggles and blamed it on her unrealistic expectations. Isn't that interesting?

As she spoke, her story came alive in the most beautiful way.

Rebekah's entire life, all she wanted was to be a wife and mom. She thought it was the perfect job for her to use all of her skills, a perfect fit for her personality, and was truly the desire of her heart.

She married the love of her life, but due to circumstances beyond their choices, they had to postpone their plans of starting a family. During her waiting, she began to further idealize what life would be like once they started having children. Rebekah described her vision of motherhood as sitting in the rocking chair in a striking but simple nursery, nursing her newborn while wearing a long, flowing, white cotton gown. The windows were open and the handmade curtains she hung were billowing in the breeze. The picture of perfection. As she was describing her vision to me, it felt like I was in that perfect moment of motherhood with her, and it sounded so nice. (Also, very much unlike my reality.)

Fast forward to the days when Rebekah's dream came true. She became a mother to a sweet, perfect baby boy – but her vision of what motherhood would be like was nowhere in sight. Reality set in, and she quickly realized how difficult the newborn days truly are, and they were nothing like the life she had daydreamed about for years. Rebekah was crushed. She had longed for this life for so long, and she had spent her waiting period building it up in her mind. When her reality looked *so* different from her dreams, she felt like a failure, and it broke her heart.

Of course, she was not a failure. Rebekah went on to have more children, and she is one of the most amazing mothers I've ever met. She is a kindhearted and gentle woman who loves the Lord in a way that lights up her spirit. I am so happy to have her in my life, and I'm happy that I could share part of her story with you.

Is there something in Rebekah's story that you could take and apply to your life? Is there some unrealistic expectation you've been holding onto, to the point that it's breaking your heart?

If you struggle with feeling like you've lost yourself in motherhood, does it have anything to do with unrealistic expectations of what you thought motherhood would be like?

Sometimes we choose to let things rob us of our peace.

Yes, choose.

Jesus left us His peace, and it is vastly different from the peace the world offers. Whereas all the world really can offer is a daydream, Jesus offers true peace that passes all understanding. He offers divine comfort and sweet nurturing in exchange for our fears.

We can choose to embrace the peace Jesus gave to us or we can choose to embrace the doubts, fear, and disappointments the devil presents before us as an option that only looks like the truth.

Jesus says "Let not your heart be troubled" in the New King James Version of John 14:27.

What an interesting way of phrasing it.

"Let not."

Do not let.

Let.

If you *let* someone into your house, you willing accept them as guests. If you *let* the dog outside, you are encouraging him to go into the yard. If you *let* yourself out, you choose to leave. If you *let* your child eat their dessert first, you are giving them permission. If you *let* go of something, you make the choice not to hold onto it.

The word "let" implies a choice and an action.

So, what if we make a better choice?

Do not *let* your heart be troubled by unrealistic expectations.

In other words, do not allow it to happen.

God has given us everything we need to make a better choice. We can lean on Him. We can call out the devil's lies for what they are. We can choose joy. We can pick up the peace that Jesus left for us. We can invite the Holy Spirit to do what Jesus promised – to teach us and remind us of everything we need to know.

The key is to spend as much time in the scriptures as we possibly can. I know life is busy, I know it's hard. But I also know it's worth it. My friend Rebekah would tell you it's worth it, too.

Psalm 119 says in verse 11 "I have hidden your word in my heart, that I might not sin against you" (NLT).

How do we do that, though? How do we hide things in our heart?

It comes with soaking ourselves in the scriptures. We must be reading the Bible and prayerfully asking God to hide His words in our hearts and asking the Holy Spirit to stir those words up when we need them! The Holy Spirit can only remind us of the things we've already put into our hearts. It's up to us to actually make the effort. That is the work we must do so that our key verse for today can help us go full circle. That is the work we must do so that we are relying on God and His truths to be our foundation, instead of fueling ourselves with daydreams and unrealistic expectations that will only lead to disappointment. Jesus promised us a different kind of peace. Will you reach out and take it? Are you willing to do your part?

Prayer Journal Prompt

Jesus, thank You for leaving me the peace You knew my heart would so desperately need. I've been holding onto unrealistic expectations for too long, and it's damaging my life, my motherhood experience, and keeping me from experiencing joy. I give it all to You. Adjust me, help me with ...

Day 16:

 Found Wonderfully Made

Psalm 139:13-14 NLT

You made all the delicate, inner parts of my body and knit me together in my mother's womb. Thank you for making me so wonderfully complex! Your workmanship is marvelous – how well I know it.

This verse is used a lot for new babies, and it makes sense. It's *so easy* to praise God for the babies He gave us to love. But hold on just a minute…

This Psalm was written by King David, and he wasn't writing about his child(ren). *He was writing this about himself.*

I can look at my son and think so many wonderful things about him. I tell him that he is brave, smart, sweet, loving, strong-willed, the list goes on and on. I can look at my daughter and remember my recent pregnancy with her. I can marvel at the way God created life and allowed my womb to be a part of something so incredible. But the minute somebody compliments *me*, I get kind of uncomfortable.

If someone were to ask you, what would you say makes you wonderful? How quickly would you have an answer?

Wonderful is a pretty strong word. Even if you aren't a person who struggles with self-love or confidence, even if you are at total ease under a compliment, can you rattle off a list of what makes you wonderful the same way you can if someone asked you what makes your kids wonderful?

As moms, it's natural for this verse to remind us of our own babies just because of the words "mother's womb." We relate to it. Those words remind us of an experience that changes our lives and our families forever.

On a side note, I really believe that God has tucked various verses all throughout the Bible that are especially for certain people. That's not to say that the Bible isn't for everyone – please don't misunderstand what I'm trying to say. But I think that there are some verses in here that God put here just for us, just for the mamas. This verse... even though it was written by King David, who was a man, I believe these were inspired thoughts that God deposited into him to write and share. The Bible, cover to cover, is God-breathed. Regardless of who wrote what, the words came from God. The human author was just the vessel. While everyone can read the verse, nobody else can understand and feel the weight of what a "mother's womb" means quite like a woman with a womb.

Digressing, a bit, let's return to the focus, this verse isn't about the mother or the babies in our wombs (or our arms, laps, or living rooms), it's about the adult that God knit together a long time ago, in another womb.

It's about *you.*

Use this space to rewrite this verse, subbing in your name for words like "me" and "I" to make it feel even more personable.

It's not conceited to know that God made you, and that He only makes amazing things.

God made you amazing.

He artfully crafted you.

And what's more than that, consider this:

 First, He made you.
Then He made you a mom.

Years ago, God knit you together with a little of this, a little of that. He made you from the inside out. He gave you talents, gifts, passions, flaws, cravings... He set the foundation for everything you would ever become. *And then* He gave you your kids. He gave those children to you, knowing full well who you were.

Maybe you've been inclined to feel like you've lost yourself because you don't do many of the things you once loved. Perhaps the majority of your time is spent caring for children, your house, your husband, and it seems like that's all you have time for. I think we all go through those seasons.

I was probably feeling the most burnt out as a mom when I wasn't doing the things that were life-giving to me. Most importantly, I wasn't in the Word regularly.

It's easy to slip into feeling like we have lost who we are when we are living day in and day out without the reminders of who God says we are.

Without that basic need being filled, there certainly was a gap in my life. And that gap gave the devil just enough room to weasel in and widen that gap further by whispering doubts and grievances into my ear. My unprotected mind was all too quick to gobble up what

> *Mama, you are in a season of life that is so precious and so valuable, and you deserve to feel content.*

sounded true at the time. I loved my life as a new mom, and I was so happy with my baby. But I was still searching for a way to feel like me. This is something I know moms can understand universally. Only a mom can feel so whole and so empty all at the same time.

As we talked about in an earlier devotion, Found Fighting, we have to put on the armor of God and fortify our minds against the sneaky schemes from the enemy.

Mama, you are in a season of life that is so precious and so valuable, and you deserve to feel content.

I can tell you about my own experience. As my son got a little older and wasn't a newborn anymore, I started finding ways to bring myself back into my motherhood path. Making time in my day to spend with Jesus made a world of difference. Making time – forcing an opening in my day and being intentional was and continues to be key. This fueled my soul in so many ways and with my heart full of gratitude, I had a little more energy to give.

My personal story, in regard to feeling lost and what the solution was for me, is actually kind of ironic. I have been a creative soul my entire life. As a little girl, I declared I would be a writer. As I got older, I began thinking that writing was kind of weird, so I kept my journal habits private and started painting instead. When my son was a baby and wet paint didn't seem practical, I switched to baking cakes and breads to sell in my community to pad the budget when I first became a stay-at-home mom. Oh, was I searching. I started a network marketing business soon after that and poured massive amounts of time and effort and energy into searching out ideas and turning them into pretty graphics and heartfelt written posts. My soul longed for a creative outlet, and I didn't start feeling like I had found it until I really dove into the Bible, spent ample amounts of time praying over the situation, and hearing from God as to what He wanted me to do. I think you can figure out what happened next. Here I am, writing this book. He brought me full circle, and I've never felt more found than I do now, because I've found the calling God has on my life in this season – called to motherhood, called to serve Him by serving my family, and called to use my gifts for Him by writing this book. I am fearfully and wonderfully made for this life and for serving my King and stepping into that truth has made a huge difference in my life.

Ephesians 2:10 NLT says "For we are God's masterpiece. He has created us anew in Christ Jesus, so we can do the good things he planned for us long ago."

Mama-Sister-Friend, there is something God has prepared for you to do. He knit together the groundwork for you to step into the things He called you to before you were even born.

You are just as wonderfully made as the babies you grew, and you have a wonderful purpose assigned to you by the One who created you. More than that, you won't feel fully at peace until you find out what it is and *do it*.
I tell you all the time that you aren't lost in motherhood, but perhaps you still have some *finding* to do.

In any event, don't forget the words of King David —
I am fearfully and wonderfully made.

Prayer Journal Prompt

Lord, I want to be the best mom I can be. I have felt like something is missing from my life, and I don't want to feel that way anymore. Help me find my one-of-a-kind calling. Show me what good work You have already prepared for me to complete. I want to love myself by filling this gap in my life in a way that pleases You. I want to *feel* like I'm wonderfully made by fulfilling the calling You have for me. Show me what it is You have for me to do to fulfill my purpose. Give me strength and courage and boldness in ...

Day 17:

 Avoiding Burn Out

1 Corinthians 15:58 NLT

So, my dear brothers and sisters, be strong and immovable. Always work enthusiastically for the Lord, for you know that nothing you do for the Lord is ever useless.

Some people say we get burnt out when we are trying to do too much. There's a popular idea right now that boils down to moms needing self-care to solve all their problems. I'm not knocking self-care, but I am definitely questioning *most* of the ways the world tells us to care for ourselves.

There was a viral post circulating social media a few years ago, and it ruffled my feathers then, and I guess you could say my feathers continue to be ruffled. The post listed all the things that are *not* self-care for moms. The list included things like going grocery shopping alone, taking a shower or going to the bathroom by yourself. It went on to list other things that the writer considered to be basic human rights and therefore did not count as self-care. The reason it annoyed me is because I regarded some of those things as acts of self-care because they felt refreshing to me! If going to the grocery store by myself and enjoying that time feels restorative to me, who says it doesn't count?

It got me thinking about self-care. As Christians, we have to remember that the Lord is where we find ultimate rest. He is the great redeemer, and He is where we can find true restoration. Spending time with Him is the greatest and most complete act of self-care in existence.

Mama, isn't the goal of self-care to avoid being burnt out? What if we were intentionally living our lives *with* joy instead of living life and then trying to supplement joy after the fact? Living a life pleasing to God and fulfilling the unique callings He has chosen and placed on us is how we avoid feeling burnt out. So much of our self-care is us trying to do damage control.

While I love taking a hot Epsom salt bath, or doing my workout alone, and yes, I do love grocery shopping by myself, and a day at the spa sounds absolutely lovely – and there's nothing wrong with those things – but they aren't meant to take the place of time with the Savior. There's a cross-shaped hole in each of our hearts, and only Jesus can make us whole.

Our verse for today is from 1 Corinthians, so it's part of a letter that Paul wrote to the church In

Corinth. The church in Corinth was struggling, but they *were* Christians. They were Christians in a city that we could compare in moral value to New Orleans or Las Vegas or maybe my Myrtle Beach, here in my home state of South Carolina. Paul's instructions in today's key verse are coming at the end of a passage about Jesus coming back and securing the final victory. In the meantime, in the waiting time, we are to be always working for the Lord, and Paul promises it won't be in vain. It's like he is telling us that the work God gives us is important and reminding us to not give up. Keep going. Don't succumb to the burn out and don't put too much weight on worldly solutions while skipping over the relief God can offer.

Let's talk about a few practical ways to avoid feeling burnt out.

❃ Staying in the Word.

Just read your Bible. There are obstacles, I know. Resolve to overcome them. Acknowledge that the devil will do anything to keep you out of the Bible and distant from God and be determined to *not* let him win. We always make room in our lives for the things that are most important to us, so I challenge you to make this a top priority. Romans 11:16, one of my favorite verses in the Bible because it applies to so many aspects of our life, says "And since

Abraham and the other patriarchs were holy, their descendants will also be holy – just as the entire batch of dough is holy because the portion given as an offering is holy. For if the roots of the tree are holy, the branches will be, too" (NLT). This is a beautiful and compelling scripture that speaks to our need to spend time in the Word of God while also showing us the way it can impact our children and our children's children. Reading the Bible is the most uplifting, inspiring, convicting, and educational experience. It's packed full of encouragement that God knows we need to help us through every situation we encounter – including feeling burnt out, sometimes. I can't encourage you enough to find out what the Bible has for you during those seasons that you feel burnt out, even the seasons when you're so burnt you're crispy. What a gift we've been given – a book that is *alive.* A book that you can open and somehow find the perfect verse at the perfect time. See what it has for you!

✳ Talking to Jesus.

Y'all, we overthink things so much! Just talk to Jesus! He wants to hear from you – nothing is too big or too small for Him to care about. It doesn't matter if you talk to Him silently in your heart and mind, or if you pray out loud. It doesn't matter if you are multi-tasking and praying while you do your chores or giving your kids a bath. It doesn't matter if you pray yourself to sleep – that means you're finding comfort in your Heavenly Father. 1 Thessalonians 5:17 (NLT) says "Never stop praying." Praying all the time is what will help us avoid burn out, because we'll be taking our problems to God immediately; instead of letting them fester inside of us until they become unbearable. If you have trouble staying focused, try starting a prayer journal. I don't mean these journaling pages I've included for you; I mean starting your own empty-notebook prayer journal and just spilling your guts out to the Lord on those pages. Talk to Jesus. Tell Him how you feel. Let His peace wash over you. Nothing can cure that burnt out feeling the way Jesus can.

❋ Leaning on Christian friends.

If you don't have any Christian friends that you can talk to, go to with prayer requests, confide in, and pray with – then that's your next mission in life. Some ways to find friends who are believers are going to church, getting involved in serving, joining a small group or a Bible study. Be choosy. Jesus says in Matthew 7:21, "Not everyone who calls out to me, 'Lord! Lord!' will enter the Kingdom of Heaven. Only those who actually do the will of my Father in heaven will enter" (NLT). Unfortunately, not everyone who claims to be a Christian is also a follower of the will of God. We need to be surrounded by people who love God and point us to God because that is where they are going. Everything is easier in life when you have a buddy who gets it. Just as if you are doing a new diet or healthy eating plan with a friend, it's easier to have an accountability partner. Maybe you're seeking sobriety – it's a little easier if you're walking with others who have gone before you and found success. The same is true with leaning on and having trustworthy Christian friends. Having someone to point us to Jesus and pray for us when we are feeling burnt out is literally life changing. Lean on your Christian friends, pour into the relationships in your life that have potential to become those Christian friendships. If you don't have Christian friends, spend some time today praying that God will send you some.

✳ Listening to worship music.

Confession time – I used to hate praise and worship music. I grew up listening to classic rock and after studying music history in college, fell in love with music from the 1960's and 1970's. Changing the radio from a song that I loved to a praise and worship station where, to me, everything sounded the same and I didn't know the words to any of the songs, was tough. I started simple in my transition of music. When my son was being particularly difficult or when I was faced with some sort of stress, I would listen to praise and worship music. It started out as just listening for a song or two. As time went on, I don't know how to describe it, but the lyrics started burrowing down into my heart. I started to learn the songs, even started liking some of the songs. I found myself worshiping and praying though hard moments with the help of these songs. I stand before you as a recovering-praise-and-worship-music-hater and want to encourage you to do a little listening to some praise music in your own life when you're having a hard moment or when you're feeling burnt out. We were made to worship, and the more time we spend worshipping, the less time we'll have for wallowing.

❊ Finding a way to zone out that pleases God.

The whole point is to just turn to God, give everything to Jesus.

We have so many options of other things we can turn to when we are feeling stressed, conflicted, or just plain burnt out. Instead of turning to other things like scrolling social media, playing a game on your phone, listening to music that doesn't point us to Jesus, instead of reading or watching something you'd be ashamed to watch with Jesus in the room, instead of turning to drugs or alcohol (and I say that because I've been there and turned to those things), I want to challenge you to find a way to zone out that *pleases* God.

Those feelings of burn-out are going to come. If we *need* to turn to Jesus, even neutral activities become problematic when we use them to zone out instead of going to God. Suddenly, the harmless thing isn't so harmless anymore. The relief, at best, will only be temporary because God designed us to need Him. Putting off the problem isn't the same thing as finding a solution. As mothers, we are uniquely poised to provide our children with such a beautiful example of how to handle life's problems as they roll into our lives. If your children can see you read a book or pick up your phone, they can see you pick up your Bible. If they can hear you tuning into your favorite old song to zone out, they can hear you crank up the praise music and take a moment with the Lord. There are countless ways to zone out that please God. Maybe you need to get creative, and that is okay, too. Do you like to bake when you're stressed? How can you use that to please God? Maybe you bake something to give away and use it as an opportunity to show love to a neighbor. Maybe you like to listen to podcasts when you need a mental break – so try listening to a podcast that reads the Bible to you while you carry on with your day. If you can find a way to avoid that burnt out feeling from taking over and getting you too burnt, too crispy, that's good! But if you can do that in a way that pleases God, brings glory to Him and His kingdom, and provides your family with an example of how to handle their own feelings of overwhelm? That is more than good. That is beautiful.

Our key verse for today wraps everything up nicely with the bow of reminding you that the work you put in for God is never useless. Read it again. Hold onto that verse like a life raft if you are teetering on the edge. God does not want you to feel hopeless – not when He offers so much hope.

Prayer Journal Prompt

Lord, Sometimes I just get to the end of my rope and feel so burnt out on everything. I don't want to feel burnt out, and I want help me get through seasons of burn out by turning to You instead of …

Day 18:

The Good Ol' Days

Ecclesiastes 7:10 NIV

Do not say, "Why were the old days better than these?" For it is not wise to ask such questions.

A few years ago, I showed my husband an advertisement for a simple wooden sign that stopped me in my tracks. The sign read, "These are the good old days." Today, these words are on display in our living room. They sit up high, carved into white wood, and oversee toys, snuggles, and tantrums alike.

The gentle words are an invitation to enjoy *these* days, a reminder not to take them for granted and let them slip away, and a subtle nod (for me) to Ecclesiastes 7:10, our verse for today.

I know, I know. It is just *so tempting* sometimes to think back about life before motherhood and just daydream a little. What do you remember the most about life before you became a mama? How would you describe it? What name would you give that season?

I think I would give my past name, 'Freedom Days.'

The thing I remember the most fondly is the lack of responsibility. The responsibilities of motherhood are on such a different level that the responsibilities before pale in comparison.

It might break my heart, but I'll be free.

Sure, there's a motherload (pun thoroughly intended) of responsibility packed into *these* days, but they're responsibilities that give my life so much of its meaning – even while pushing my limits and making me long for the days when I felt free. I'll be free again someday. It might break my heart, but I'll be free. One day, the season I'm in now will be a memory and I have a feeling I'll find myself pining over the sometimes-maddening weight of what it meant to be a tiny person's everything. One day I will sit in silence and miss the good ol' days I'm living out right now. (Today's verse will apply then, too.)

For now, we can heed the Biblical advice in our key verse today by remembering that there's not a single chapter of life that is meant to last forever. If we use valuable energy pining over days gone by, we miss out on *these* days as they're passing. It would be far wiser to appreciate the days as they roll in and out and recognize even the hardest parts as being just that – a part.

This is just a season.

In spite of the hard, in spite of the messy, in spite of the new levels of exhaustion we keep seeming to unfold, in spite of the things that go wrong, in spite of the derailed plans, in spite of it all... these are the good ol' days.

The days before were not better. Maybe they were cleaner, easier, and simpler– but they weren't better. They were just different. I fully believe that this verse is one of those verses that the Lord tucked into His Holy Scriptures as a reminder just for us moms. Just for you, when He knew you would need a reminder to enjoy these days for what they are and to not dwell on the days gone by.

Prayer Journal Prompt ·

Lord, I'm guilty of spending too much time daydreaming about the past and taking the blessings of today for granted. Forgive me. Today I want to thank You for my life and ask for help in

...

Day 19:

Found Faithful

2 Thessalonians 3:3 NLT

But the Lord is faithful; he will strengthen you and guard you from the evil one.

We schedule so many parts of our lives. Everything from appointments to dinner plans to playdates. While motherhood absolutely requires a certain amount of flexibility, there are some constants to our days. Maybe the one and only thing you can depend on every day is that first cup of coffee, or maybe you follow a tight daily itinerary – whatever it may be, to some degree, we all have a schedule or at least a daily rhythm that we follow. There are things we depend on.

Today I want to remind you that the number one thing we can depend on is God's faithfulness. He is faithful. He will *always* be found faithful. The Bible is full of examples, but I want to challenge you to look over your life and find your own personal examples of His faithfulness and goodness. They are there, even in the most destitute times. Remember? What we look for, we will find!

We can count on Him for countless things, but my next question is ... can He count on us showing up in the relationship? I can just imagine Him sitting at the table in the kitchen, hands folded and faithfully, patiently waiting while we bustle around. He shows up. Do we?

Do we schedule Him into our daily lives? Are *we* faithful?

There's an expression that goes something like, "if the devil can't make you bad, he'll make you busy." It really speaks to me because I feel like I'm at a point in my life where I don't encounter a lot of temptation that would pull me away from Jesus. I'm not tempted in the same ways I was in my younger years. *But* that doesn't mean I'm not tempted away from God by a busy schedule. In fact, this is why I started writing Jesus' name at the top of my daily to-do list, even though spending time with Him has been a regular part of my daily schedule for a few years now. The devil loves to throw me for some loops first thing in the morning, because that's the part of my day that I've committed to give the Lord. It's easy to get busy, and that's why it's important for me to make a schedule. I have a daily to-do list I'm sharing with you after today's prayer journal prompt so that you can use it as you wish – maybe as a template for your own list, feel free to make copies, or there is a downloadable version on my website if you'd rather print one out. There is information in the back of this book on accessing your free download as my way of thanking you for being a found mama. For me, it's necessary to have this type of schedule. I want to be the kind of Christian that God knows He can count on to show up for Him – but it takes clear, specific effort on my part and even still, I'm not always successful.

Maybe it seems ridiculous that after almost five years of spending time with God, I still have to write it down on my daily schedule. I do this because if I don't, it might not happen. Honestly, even with it being on my daily schedule it *still* doesn't happen sometimes. And oh, my friend, it is such a desire of my heart. I know you are here because spending time with God is a desire of your heart, too. So, be encouraged to continue making your best efforts to be found faithful and know that even when your efforts end with a big belly flop, you aren't alone.

Let this serve as a reminder to keep going! Do not be discouraged on those days when you just cannot sit down. Try another method to fill in the gap (like a podcast or listening to worship music while you go about whatever has derailed your plans). Then, tomorrow, be found faithful again. Make a plan.

We know God is faithful. We know this because He has proven Himself over and over again in our own lives, and we know this because the Bible tells us it is true. He makes us stronger, and every time we successfully give Him portions of our days, it solidifies this daily habit and strengthens the truths of His word in our hearts.

More than that, every time we give God a portion of our day and surrender our time to Him, it's victory over the devil and all of the distractions he tries to throw between us and our Jesus.

Our faithfulness to Him gives us front row seats to witness His faithfulness in our lives and allows us to witness His strength and protection. What plans do you make to be found faithful?

Prayer Journal Prompt·

Dear God, Today I just want to thank You for the goodness, mercy, and faithfulness You've shown me. Reveal to me the pockets of time in my day that I could give to You instead of giving over to other things. Help me to schedule You into my day and establish good habits that reflect the love I have for You in my heart. You've been faithful when/through ...

Daily to-do's

Monday
- [ ] Jesus
- [ ] dinner=

Tuesday
- [ ] Jesus
- [ ] dinner=

Wednesday
- [ ] Jesus
- [ ] dinner=

Thursday
- [ ] Jesus
- [ ] dinner=

Friday
- [ ] Jesus
- [ ] dinner=

Weekend
- [ ] Jesus
- [ ] dinner=

Proverbs 25:1

Day 20:

Found Still

Psalm 46:10 NLT

"Be still, and know that I am God! I will be honored by every nation. I will be honored throughout the world."

I opened my Bible this morning, unsure of what the Lord had for me today, and when I saw this verse highlighted in my pages, I knew I had to tell you a story about this Bible verse. This is an important verse to my family because it reminds us of my mom's brush with death.

Join me, if you will, for a tale that takes place deep in the woods of South Carolina.

Picture a small, three-red light town. It's the remnants of what was once a thriving little place, nestled just an hour from the beach. Palm trees line the road where houses and businesses alternate between tidy and neglected. Now, drive fifteen minutes out of town. You turn towards a public boat landing on a dead-end road. Off of that road, you drive down a half mile gravel road that opens up to a small clearing in the woods with only four homes. One of those houses is mine and my husband's home. The house next door is where I grew up and where my parents still live. We've traded cell-phone service and conveniences for a serene little nook in nature. Our houses sit on top of a fairly steep hill, and at the very bottom of the incline is some swampy water on the edge of a lake that floods with overflow from a nearby river.

At the time, I was at work 40 minutes away. Everyone else was at work, too – my dad, my sister, my husband, and most of our neighbors. My mom was home alone. She was spending the day doing something completely normal and ordinary for her, she was working in the yard, utilizing my Daddy's tractor. We all used his tractor pretty regularly and we all were familiar with proper tractor safety, including my mom. So, my mom is out in the back yard working near the top of the hill. She parked the tractor, thought she set the parking brake because it was on a slight incline, and she hopped off to go about her work. When she saw the tractor beginning to roll backwards down the hill, she tried to stop it. Now, I know that sounds silly, but who would just watch an expensive piece of machinery roll away down a hill towards some water and not try to do anything? So, she runs after the slowly rolling tractor and jumps on with the intention of pulling the parking brake before the tractor rolls any further.

This is where our story goes horribly wrong.

The tractor has gained too much momentum. It cannot be stopped.

As it rolls, it gains speed and flips, throwing my mother off of the tractor and flying through the air. She lands further down the hill and in an instant, the tractor is right there. As it's flipping and tumbling down the hill, it lands on top of her – bouncing off of her and rolling over her on its way as it barrels down the hill.

It was a traumatic, horrendous accident, but the worst was not over.

My mom couldn't get up. She knew she was badly hurt. When Momma retells her story, she says she had no fear that day. Even after the accident, she was overwhelmed with peace and fully convinced she was going to meet Jesus that day. The only sadness in her heart was for what her family would see when we got home, and she was gone to Glory.

She tried to belly crawl and pull herself up the hill with her arms, but it wasn't possible. She says she felt God whisper to her, "Be still and know that I'm your God." So that's what she did. She laid there still for a long, long while.

This all happened shortly after one o'clock, when my dad had just gone back to work after coming home for lunch. Nobody was home. There was no one around to help. Momma was yelling for help, but the wind blew her cries back towards her and she knew that no one could hear her. She begged the dogs to go get help, but they just lay beside her, keeping her company.

She lay there on the hill for *four hours*. That will never stop breaking my heart when I think about it.

Shortly after five o'clock, Daddy got home from work and went inside their empty house. Daddy called for her in the house and got no answer, so he went looking for her. That was when he saw the tractor at the bottom of the hill. I can't imagine the panic he must have felt in that moment. He ran to look for her and found her lying on the hill – broken, dirty, and wounded. He ran back to the house to call 911. It took the ambulance a while to get to our house. They couldn't find us. Again, we live in a very remote area and even GPS isn't always reliable for finding our houses.

I can remember my sister calling me at work and telling me that Momma had been run over by the tractor. To this day, my family loves to give me a hard time because my reaction was to laugh. You see, my mom is very accident-prone. In the years prior, she had broken her foot twice just walking around the house. She was always having silly little accidents that often involved her feet. So, when they told me she was run over by a tractor, I just assumed it was her foot. My sister was also at work, but she had talked to our dad. She didn't know the specifics, but said she thought it was bad and we needed to get home. I was finishing up at work anyway, and said I'd meet her there.

I was on my way home when my husband called me. He had already made it home. I can remember everything about this moment. He told me the paramedics were still deciding whether they were going to take her to the nearest trauma hospital, or if they were going to call the medivac helicopter to take her a few hours away to the medical university in Charleston, South Carolina.

I had to pull over in the median as I was driving. I instantly became hysterical. I remember hyperventilating. I was a complete mess. This was obviously not another broken foot and the realization of that hit me like a ton of bricks.

I had to sit there and wait until the emergency responders further evaluated my mom's condition because one hospital was north, the other hospital was south, and I was right in the middle.

Thankfully, they decided she wasn't wounded badly enough to require the helicopter and took her to the nearest trauma center. I remember little of that drive.

When I arrived, they let me go see my mom in the emergency room. When I saw my Momma laying on that table, surrounded by nurses and doctors working to evaluate her injuries ... well, I lost it. Again.

My mom, being her truest self, was fully awake and *she* began comforting *me*. If you could meet us, you'd know this is just *exactly* like my mom and just *exactly* like me.

The injuries she sustained that day included a broken back in three places, a broken rib, and her pelvis had more breaks than they could count.

She was in the hospital for a week.

After she was discharged from the hospital, she moved into a rehabilitation nursing home facility. My capable and energetic mom, at the ripe age of 49, in any kind of nursing facility was not something I could wrap my brain around. When she finally came home, she brought with her an elaborate back brace that wrapped around her entire torso that she had to wear every waking moment for the next two months. The accident had claimed her independence, and she couldn't be left alone. She couldn't even stand without assistance and used a walker to get around the short distances required.

My mom went on to make a full recovery, and mere words can't express how grateful I am that the Lord let us keep my Momma that day. Otherwise, she would have been absent from so many memories - most especially, the fact that she would have never met her three grandchildren had she met Jesus that day.

Like I said at the beginning, today's key verse is *special* to my family. Anytime I come across it, I think about the day she almost died beneath an out-of-control tractor barreling down a steep hill. I share this story with you because I saw the verse in my Bible this morning and knew I was supposed to share her story – a story I cannot retell without tears burning in my eyes.

Psalm 44:25-26 says "We collapse in the dust, lying face down in the dirt. Rise up! Help us! Ransom us because of your unfailing love" (NLT).

What a beautiful way to describe gravity, the same gravity that almost claimed by mom's life. My mom's story is one of redemption. It's a tale about

God not being done with her yet. She turned to Him that day, and His love didn't fail her.

Whatever your hardest thing is – that most difficult circumstance in your life, the thing that you think is over and God can't fix, the things that brings you crumbling down to the dust, the thing that sometimes feels like it's killing you – sometimes the only thing there is for us to do is, be still.

Know that God is God and that He *will* be exalted. His love is unfailing.

Be still.

Find yourself sitting still in the presence of the Lord today. Sit with God. Give your troubles and worries to Him, whatever they may be – no matter how big or small.

Prayer Journal Prompt

God, sometimes I realize I just need to be still and let You be God. This devotion today made me think about …

Day 21:

Found Frustrated

Romans 8:26 NLT

And the Holy Spirit helps us in our weakness. For example, we don't know what God wants us to pray for. But the Holy Spirit prays for us with groanings that cannot be expressed in words.

I write this book in the mornings as I sip my coffee. It's one of my favorite parts of the day. I sit down at the breakfast table with my son. He eats breakfast and watches cartoons while I work. I have out my laptop, my Bible, and notebooks. There are some mornings when I feel like I could sit here all day, reading, reflecting, writing.

But I am a mom. In addition to staying home with my son at the time of this writing, I was also keeping my best friend's son while she taught school. Our boys are about the same age. My lifelong friend and I live only a few minutes apart. We now delight in our sons growing up together - the makings of another lifelong friendship.

Our two boys keep me on my toes. As much as I would love to sit and tap away at these keys until the sun goes down, that's not the season of life I'm in. I'm a mama, I'm also a wife, a homemaker, a daughter, a sister, a granddaughter, and a friend. I'm realizing right now that our house has a revolving door with loved ones popping in and out for visits and play dates. I've always wanted to have one of "those" houses and it looks like that dream has come true, but I'm telling you that to illustrate that *there's a lot going on over here.*

While I wouldn't have it any other way, can you imagine why I might have titled this devotional "Found Frustrated"? There are plenty of things in my life that could easily be a source of frustration.

Just a side note: I am laughing at myself right now. I *had intended* to sit down and write about all the things that went wrong yesterday, and yet while I was setting the context, instead I rattled off the blessings ... on accident. I was just trying to set up some context for my complaint. (Thank you, Holy Spirit in the middle of my writing you remind me of my blessings. You're good like that.)

So, dear friend, back to my original point. We all have frustrating days, frustrating moments, times when it feels like the devil is just throwing wrenches at us over every little thing. It makes us want to scream. I have days like that, too! Yesterday started out like that for me *before* the sun was even fully up over the trees in our backyard. Things go wrong – big things and small things – and it can leave us feeling cranky, frustrated, and just *done*. #overit

How many times have you just thrown up your hands and said, "I'm so done with this!"

Done with the children not listening, done with arguing and explaining and answering the never-ending question of "Why?", done with messes being made faster than they can get cleaned up, just done. *All done.*

And how do we even pray for these things? They're so trivial, but God still cares.

Lord, I'm just cranky today and need some help.

Lord, I'm just all done and there's still so much day left ahead of me – help me keep going.

Lord, I'm just so frustrated!

I love the part of our verse from Romans today that references the Holy Spirit groaning out prayers for us. Sometimes my prayers have been not much more than a groan! Sharing your problems with God isn't something we do to remind Him of what we're going through. He already knows, but when we tell Him about our problems, we're reminding ourselves that God is bigger than anything we face.

Sometimes, we are so struck in our frustrations that we don't even have it within our scopes to pray for the things we truly need to pray for, and He still is bigger than even that. God is not limited by our prayers. God is not boxed in by what we think we need to pray for.

I love our verse for today because it reminds me that even when I'm not praying rightly, Jesus hears and makes even the mess I pray righteous. Maybe I'm praying about my frustrations, and I need to be asking for gratitude. Maybe I'm praying about my bad mood, and I should be asking God what He's trying to teach me. Maybe I'm praying for my kid who isn't listening and telling God all about it, and I should be praying about why the enemy is attacking and praying a hedge of protection around my family. Or maybe God is using my child to show me how frustrated He gets when *I* am the one *not listening*.

I don't want to be a cranky mom, but the truth is, sometimes I am. You too?

But – and this is the beautiful part, Mama-Sister-Friend – the Holy Spirit has us covered. He prays to God, The Father, *for* us when our prayers miss the mark. We have weaknesses, and the Holy Trinity knows all about it and there is a system in place to take care of us. God's provisions don't stop where our prayers do. There are prayers being offered up for us by the Holy Spirit *that are perfect prayers,* and they fill in the gaps that our imperfections so often leave.

Prayer Journal Prompt

God, You know the frustrations in my life. You know the things that make me cranky and unpleasant. You see the weaknesses in my life, and You know the prayers I should be praying but are left overlooked. I am so weak, You are so strong, and Lord, today I just want to pray for all of it. The things I'm done with, the things I need that I don't even know how to put into words. I want my prayers to align with the prayers of the Holy Spirit. Show me how to pray and what to pray for. I am feeling led today to pray about ...

Day 22:

 The Coffee Tastes Better When He Makes It

Isaiah 55:8-9 NLT

"My thoughts are nothing like your thoughts,"
says the LORD. "And my ways are far beyond
anything you could imagine. For just as the
heavens are higher than earth, so my ways are
higher than your ways and my thoughts higher
than your thoughts."

My husband always sets up the coffee pot at night
so that when we wake up the next morning, hot
coffee is waiting for us. At some point, as an
attempt at an act of service towards my husband, I
took over making the coffee. I wanted to take one
of his daily tasks on as his helper, and I just started
setting up the coffee pot when I cleaned up the
kitchen after dinner.

But one night I had a revelation.

Before our second child, our daughter, came along,
we had what we called "Date Night In" every
Thursday. Our son hangs out with my parents for a
few hours and eats dinner with them. This is an
idea we borrowed from someone else, and it's
been the greatest thing. If possible, I highly

recommend a regularly scheduled date-night-in. It's so relaxing and I love to hang out and catch up with my husband. One Thursday night, we were really invested in a movie and lost track of time, making us late to go get our son before his normal bedtime. I was throwing some things in the dishwasher and asked my husband if he wouldn't mind making the coffee. He said he would. But, since I had taken over making the coffee, I had been using a new scoop. He asked me how much water I put in and how many scoops I had been using. So, I literally guided him through making the coffee, and he was following my directions precisely - except for one change. He poured out just a little water and said we didn't need that much. I was doubtful but kept quiet and let judgements on how wrong he was bounce around my brain, just beneath the surface.

And I'm here to tell you, the coffee tasted better the next morning when my husband made it.

Nobody was more surprised than I was when I took that first sip.

Thinking about that, and sipping on this delicious coffee I didn't make, got me thinking about today's key verse from Isaiah.

My husband's coffee being so much tastier than the coffee I made reminds me of how God's plans are so much better than my own plans.

I had already decided that I liked the way I make coffee, and my husband's coffee probably wasn't going to taste as good. I was so sure of myself. I was so prideful.

Wouldn't life be so much sweeter if we carried this mentality over to our faith? What if we embraced God's plans for us, knowing full well that those plans *will be* better than anything we can brew up on our own? Unfortunately, many times, we like to think our way is better. We like to think we've got it all figured out. We like to think our routine is set in stone and there's no better way. But sometimes, we need minor adjustments. Sometimes we need just a little water poured out. Sometimes we just need to trust. Sometimes we need to remember what God told Isaiah when He said, "My thoughts are nothing like your thoughts."

> *What if we embraced God's plans for us, knowing full well that those plans will be better than anything we can brew up on our own?*

God's way is better. It is always better, and it will always be better.

Exponentially better.

Turn in your Bible and read Isaiah 55:8-13. These words are a beautiful and poetic reminder that if we just let God work it all out, all of heaven and earth will rejoice with us as the good plans and good thoughts of the Lord come to fruition.

The coffee will be better.

Or, we can do it our way...and deal with the thorns.

(I think this is a sign from the Lord that my husband needs to make the coffee from now on, right?)

Prayer Journal Prompt

Lord, I know Your ways are better than my ways, but sometimes I need reminding. I don't want to deal with the thorns that result from doing things my way. I want to rejoice with heaven and earth in Your goodness. Thank You for reminding me that ...

Day 23:

Making Memories

Proverbs 17:22 NKJV

A merry heart does good, like medicine,

But a broken spirit dries the bones.

As I'm sitting down to write, I'm at my kitchen table with my regular cup of coffee in one of my favorite cups. The sun is coming up. My husband is still sleeping. My toddler boy is watching one of his favorite shows while eating from his little favorite cereal bowl. Everything about this moment is regular.

Regular sure can be nice, can't it?

We had two big weekends back-to-back. Just last weekend, we were at the beach with my grandparents. I have so many memories of them taking me to the beach when I was a child. This time they rented a condo for us to spend the weekend together, and we had a wonderful time on an April beach in South Carolina. It wasn't too crowded, wasn't too hot, and wasn't too captivating – so we were able to tear ourselves away and go play at the park and attempt a round of putt-putt. We made some good memories together.

And the weekend before that, my son and I traveled five hours south with my mom, sister, and her baby to visit my other set of grandparents in Jacksonville, Florida. We spent time with them and had a full day at the zoo, making memories together. We relaxed together at their house, where I have so many fond memories from my own childhood.

We had two great weekends in a row, making memories.

But we don't have to travel or spend money or do extraordinary or extravagant things to make unique memories. We can make memories while doing completely ordinary things.

I heard once that as we grow older and start looking back over our lives, our happiest memories will be common, regular moments. We'll remember when our kitchen tables were covered in crumbs, and every seat was filled. We'll remember tickle fights, the best snuggles on the planet, and the games we used to play. We'll remember normal, everyday things because they would have happened over and over again until they were permanently seared into us. *Those* would be the things to go back and visit because time will prove that these ordinary moments built an extraordinary life.

On the other side of that same coin, though, is this reality: sometimes we get busy doing the things that keep all the plates spinning and we forget to have fun along the way. Sometimes we start thinking we've lost ourselves in motherhood, but *Found Mamas* are choosing not to accept that lie anymore. Still, it can be true that we have lost our joy, or maybe we've lost our merriness.

Now that needs a remedy. That needs some medicine before it breaks the spirits of the little ones entrusted to us.

I don't know about you, but I have been guilty of scolding my son for not being more patient as I finish up whatever I'm working on; like cooking dinner, or folding laundry, or cleaning the bathroom. (Who was the impatient one in that moment? Hmm?)

Again, let's read our verse for today. Proverbs 17:22 says, "*A merry heart does good, like medicine, But a broken spirit dries the bones*" (NKJV).

Mama-Sister-Friend, this one is easily applied to motherhood. A mama's merry heart can heal and keep a family well.

How? What does that look like, specifically?

Well, the Bible spells it all out for us if we do a little digging and practical application.

We can be joyful while completing our tasks and chores. Our joy comes from the Lord (Nehemiah 8:10), not from idleness (Proverbs 31:27). That's not exactly what the world says, is it? It is quite sad when we think we cannot be happy while we work and while we serve our families. My heart is breaking right now, as I write these words, over the way I snap at my son when I'm busy, instead of encouraging him to help me, instead of letting him see me complete my tasks with a joyful and grateful heart the way God intends (Colossians 3:23).

Psalm 16:11 says "You will show me the way of life, granting me the joy of your presence and the pleasures of living with you forever" (NLT).

I propose that if we are more intentional and our hearts are joyful and merry in the Lord, not only will *we* better for it (and found more obedient to

God and His expectation of His children), but *our children* will have better childhoods, as well.

Galatians 5:22-23 lists the fruit of the Spirit. As you read this verse below, think about two things. Think about what the opposite of these fruits are and think about how these traits can affect the type of mother you are to your child or children.

"But the Holy Spirit produces this kind of fruit in our lives: love, joy, peace, patience, kindness, goodness, faithfulness, gentleness, and self-control. There is no law against these things!" (NLT)

We can apply the fruit of the Spirit like holistic medicine. A preventative medicine that will not break the little one's spirits nor dry up these little bones we find clamoring about our feet while we do our chores.

If we embody this, if we walk with the Lord and grow in our faith and produce this fruit, the way we show up as mamas will be transformed. And this transformation will cover every area it needs to cover – including the everyday memories we are making while we do ordinary things.

Prayer Journal Prompt

Lord, my heart doesn't always feel joyful and for that, I want Your medicine. I want a remedy and I know that true joy can only come from You. Work on my heart so that ...

Day 24:

 *Hard Things*

Isaiah 41:10 NLT

Don't be afraid, for I am with you. Don't be discouraged, for I am your God. I will strengthen you and help you. I will hold you up with my victorious right hand.

Sometimes things are just especially hard. We find ourselves faced with things that were previously unimaginable, yet somehow … there we are, looking them right in the eye.

This leads me to today's devotion and how studying His word prepared me for this hard time I suddenly have found myself squared up against.

As I've been writing this book, I've taken to making dozens of notes in a little notebook I keep in my writing desk. When inspiration strikes, I jot down my idea or the Bible verse that stood out. When I am able to steal away a moment from my everyday life as a stay-at-home wife and mom, I can look back at my notes and write.

Those jotted down notes became extremely important.

Recently, I found myself staring into the eyes of one of my greatest fears, and I opened my notebook searching for notes that might help me find some relief in the Bible. I just knew something had to be in there.

I saw a note about Isaiah 41:10, and it just jumped out at me. On a page full of jumbled notes, that was what caught my eye. My Bible was open in front of me to 1 Corinthians.

I wasn't precisely sure where in the Bible to find Isaiah, other than I knew it was in the Old Testament.

SIDE NOTE: If you're surprised that someone writing a devotional doesn't have the books of the Bible memorized, don't be. I'm not perfect. I'm a student of The Word, just like you. Please view this as a reminder that God doesn't use perfect people or only call people who are "good enough" based on their credentials. He uses who He chooses.

Anyway, I know two things in that moment. I know that 1 Corinthians is in the New Testament, and I know that I want to find Isaiah in the Old Testament. I stick my finger somewhere random in the front half of my Bible. Now, I have to tell you that my Bible does not have tabs. And what do you know, Isaiah 41:10 was not only on the very page, but it was also right at my finger.

That day I wrote in my prayer journal, "If that was supposed to comfort me – well, I don't feel comforted. It feels like You're preparing me, and I don't want to feel prepared because I don't want this." Have you ever felt that way before?

Maybe, like me, you're going through a hardship and need to be reminded that God is with you today. Read our key verse again and let it be whatever God needs it to be for you right now – whether it be comfort or preparedness or a beacon signaling you to draw closer to Him. This is just one example of countless – the Bible is alive, and God speaks to us through His Word. God can still use the ugly parts of life, the hardest parts of life, and the things that scare us.

Maybe you are not going through a time of tragedy or hardship right now, but there are regular motherhood struggles aplenty, and this verse can still apply! Maybe you are feeling overwhelmed by having too many chores to do, feeling the weight of so much responsibility, and sometimes longing for simpler days. Throw in marriage and children – "Am I doing enough?" "Am I loving them enough?" "Are they happy enough?" – sister, it's *exhausting.*

Look at our key verse. You are not alone, and you do not have to do any single thing in your own strength.

The world is a broken place, and sin has corrupted what God meant for good. But we go back to this

"Am I doing enough?"
"Am I loving them enough?"
"Are they happy enough?" —
sister, it's exhausting.

verse from Isaiah and remember that God can carry us through all of it. Through the mundane and even through the things that feel like a gut punch that took our breath away. If you're going through a really

hard thing right now, I'm with you. I'm sorry. You aren't alone. God won't allow suffering without something good to come from it. This thing that overwhelms you can be for your good, and His glory. Until then, find comfort in Isaiah 41:10; and know that God will hold you up even when it feels like you're crumbling.

Prayer Journal Prompt

Lord, I know You're with me through the hard things and I know You're with me through the everyday things. Today, I need You to …

Day 25:

 Mom Tired

Jeremiah 17:21-23 NLT

This is what the Lord says: Listen to my warning! Stop carrying on your trade at Jerusalem's gates on the Sabbath day. Do not do your work on the Sabbath, but make it a holy day. I gave this command to your ancestors, but they did not listen or obey. They stubbornly refused to pay attention or accept my discipline.

There is a popular hashtag in the world right now, #momtired. The idea is that moms are just a different kind of tired than other humans on the planet.

Now listen, life is not a competition. God made us all different. Everyone is tired in their own way, but I don't know as much about those other ways. What I do know is that before I became a mom; I *thought* I was tired. Now, that thought makes me kind of giggle.

What I do know is I've never had a tired that lasted this long.

What I do know, and what I can say with complete certainty, is that moms are tired. I have a good friend, Kerri, and we talk often about the mental load of motherhood. Sure, everyone has the general tiredness that comes in at the end of a long day, but the mental load of keeping the family running is something altogether different.

Mama, it's exhausting to be the one who keeps up with everything, isn't it? You keep the world spinning, sometimes on your back. Your brain runs through a constant train of consciousness as you check items off an invisible list. You are always thinking of your family. You are the one who swoops in and saves the day with something as simple as "don't forget we have *xyz* today." You orchestrate an entire family by moving around puzzle pieces that nobody can see, and nobody can touch. Because of you, everything has a way of clicking.

Mom tired. We're tired in a way that only mothers can be. It is a special type of tiredness just for us.

But Mama, if reading these last paragraphs has made you feel *more tired,* I'd like to offer some relief. Yes, I get tired, but I've found a way to combat it as well. And yes, it involves adding one more thing to the list. Seems contrary, doesn't it?

God made us, created us, and crafted us with unique limits and needs. We can only accomplish so much. It is interesting to think that He could have made us to not need rest, but He didn't. Can you imagine what it would feel like if we never got tired? But God designed humans to specifically need to slow down and take a break. We require rest as much as we require food and water. God set it up a certain way, one might say He has all the answers. He even led by example.

If you read Genesis 1, you will read the creation story. Every day had a task, and every day God did His tasks well. Then, Genesis 2:2 says, "On the seventh day God had finished his work of creation, so he rested from all his work" (NLT).

Y'all, let that sink in. God rested. He was God! He was the Almighty. He wasn't *tired.* He didn't rest because He didn't have the energy to go on. He rested because He knew that rest was good. Maybe He even knew that his stubborn children would one day need to be able to say that even God rested. Not only did God rest, but He also commanded us to rest, too. It's commanded by our Creator because He knows something we try to ignore; we were created to NEED rest. He didn't have to make us that way, but it's by divine design that He did. Instead of leaning into His perfect plan, a plan that includes taking a break and resting and relaxing for just one day, we fight. We buck against the system designed to help us.

Imagine God saying something like this: "Hey friend, I've got the scoop. I know what you need, you just need a little rest and a little time with Me and you'll feel better. I made you to need this rest and relationship."

And while we trust God for so many things, how many Christians refuse to trust Him about the Sabbath?

We gotta have rest.

And these verses for today from Jeremiah are almost funny to me. God is saying He's told our ancestors to rest on the Sabbath, and they didn't listen either. Stubborn people, our ancestors. Do we share that gene? Do we continue to say, no I don't need any rest while burning ourselves out little by little, and then more and more? Are we trying it our own way, being unsatisfied with the results and with how we feel because we're still tired … but just continue trying it our own way?

Maybe your heart has softened toward this idea of Sabbath rest, and maybe you really do try to prioritize it. But maybe, old habits kick in on occasion and you find yourself succumbing to your defaulted busy-ness.

We do not *have* to live in a rat race. God really does have all the answers. He knows what we need because He was the one who gave us the need 'in the beginning,' as the old story goes.

Make time for Him.

There's no other way.

And if you've made it this far, you *have* been making time for Him. I'm *so* proud of you, Mama. I know firsthand how hard it can be at times. You're busy. And be warned my friend, once we start prioritizing God and making room in our schedules; you can believe that the devil is going to attack. So, I just want to encourage you in a few ways. Rest on the Sabbath as much as you can. I know it's hard, and sometimes we want to get a jump start on next weeks' chores. It's hard when we're the ones who prepare the family meals, etc. But do what you can to lighten the load on Sundays. Do what you can to either get your tasks done on Saturday or save what you can until Monday. Mom tired is no joke, but mama's need rest, too. Share your struggles and this solution of God and Sabbath and rest with a friend or loved one who might be going through the same things. Maybe you can even hold each other accountable. This isn't just for moms, even though we've talked about being "mom tired." This is for everyone. Everyone needs rest, everyone is commanded to keep the Sabbath holy.

We can't only spend our time doing things that drain us and expect not to wind up feeling drained. We have to do the things that give us life, too. Life-giving moments, life-giving activities. Let Sundays be different. Go drink your morning coffee outside, eat leftovers that day, play a game with your kids, notice the way the sun comes in through the windows at two o'clock, let the dishes pile up so that you can hear birds chirping instead of water running. Lay around and watch a movie with your kids, read a book. *Go to church*. Listen to praise and worship music all day long. Love on your family and let them love on you and for just this one day a week, don't focus on all the ways that you have to take care of them and just *be* with them. Let the beauty of the Sabbath wash over you this week and remind you that the tiredness you felt all week long was worth it for this kind of love. Rest, and watch God take care of the rest.

Lord, I'm not good at resting. There's so much to
do, and even on Sunday I find a way to stay busy
in spite of the commandment You have given me
to rest. I'm sorry for not respecting the Sabbath
the way that I should, and the level of tiredness I
feel is my fault for not resting in You the way
You've designed and asked me to do. Forgive me.
Help me to keep the Sabbath holy, help me to find
rest in You. Show me the changes in my life I
need to make in order for rest to be possible.
Even as I'm praying now, I can feel You revealing
to me that I could make time by ...

Day 26:

Wasting Time

John 15:19 NLT

The world would love you as one of its own if you belonged to it, but you are no longer part of the world. I chose you to come out of the world, so it hates you.

I've wasted a lot of my time being foolish and going against God. I've wasted time, opportunities, my talents. Let me give you one example.

I have a younger sister named Miranda, she's just shy of being 3 full years younger than me, but we were both fortunate enough to come from a family who was able to send us both to college. I went first and spent five years in college. My college experience ended with me dropping out, with the credits of a sophomore, and going to work full time as a waitress. My priorities were partying, socializing, and dating. I'm grateful to the Lord for saving me from myself before my habits and hobbies became truly out of control. The responsibility of how everything played out falls on only me. I was so broken at the end of it, but you can boil it all down to say I wasted so much time. I wasted opportunities that not everyone has available to them, and when I really think about that, it makes me feel sick.

Miranda, my sister, also spent five years in college, graduated and started her dream job as an elementary school teacher. She went to a Christian college where she knew basically nobody, and this choice gave her a protective bubble compared to the bubble I chose to live in. During that time, she made a wise choice to prioritize her education. She has something to show for her time spent in college as she graduated and pursued a career in education.

That's just one example, and there's so many aspects of our stories that I could tell you about – but the point is this: I wasted time and opportunity, and she didn't. The difference was choosing to stay close to Jesus, staying in His protective bubble.

These are extreme examples. All I know now is, I don't want to waste any more time. Maybe that's why I often find myself with too many irons in the fire, so to speak. But, as believers, we are called to use our time wisely.

We can apply this to ourselves, even in our lives as mothers, by serving God.

Mama, you are uniquely poised to serve the Kingdom of God.

Well, what does *that* mean?

"Serving His kingdom" is something Christians talk about often, but it can feel kind of vague. I suppose that's kind of the point. The vagueness covers a wide variety of things we can do to serve God and serve His kingdom. It can mean anything from taking on a service role in your church to doing something simple.

I once heard a missionary say that he packed up his life and moved to a third world country to serve God. When he arrived, he was given one job - sweeping the floor. At first, he did not feel like he was really serving God or doing anything significant. But eventually, he realized that it was a small way he could serve God and serve

Mama, you are uniquely poised to serve the Kingdom of God.

others. He got to the point where he felt content to sweep that floor for the rest of his life if that's what God thought was best for him, best for His kingdom.

If sweeping a floor can be missionary work for him, sweeping our own floors can be kingdom work for moms.

God's best for you may change and look different across different seasons of life. Assignments change. Doors open and close. And sometimes, just getting started and stepping into what God has for us to do, is just as important as the task being done. It's *through* doing these things that we begin to look different from the world. Often times, this is when the world starts to hate us. Reread our verse in John again.

A good indicator on whether we're serving God fully, is how the world receives us.

Do our lives point to Him in a public way? Do people look at us and know we belong to God? Do our actions show that we love Jesus? Do our habits insinuate that God rules our lives and our hearts? Will anyone be in heaven because of us? (I saw that on a church sign once and it sure packed a punch!)

One of the most important questions I believe a mother can ask herself is this: Am I serving God in the way I show up as a parent?

I want to challenge you to think of a way you might be wasting time, opportunity, or talent. As

Christians, we are called to be different from the world, that is, unbelievers. As mothers, we are called to disciple our children. Does the world hate you or do you fit right in, flying just slightly under the radar?

I think it's important from time to time to just consider what it is you could be doing to make *better* use of the time God has given you. I've wasted so much of my life pursuing things that were not pleasing to God. I don't want to waste any *more* of my life. I don't want you to waste yours, either. Check in with yourself today, and from time to time make sure you aren't wasting precious time.

Prayer Journal Prompt

Lord, I was created by You to serve You, and I don't want to waste any of this life You've given to me. You have blessed me with gifts and talents. I may not be serving You to the best of my ability. I want to point others to You, God, because You have changed my life. Show me how I can better use my ...

Day 27:

Like God Sent You

Isaiah 43:1 NLT

But now, O Jacob, listen to the Lord who created you. O Israel, the one who formed you says, "Do not be afraid, for I have ransomed you. I have called you by name; you are mine."

There's a quote circulating on social media right now that kind of shocked my system. It said something along the lines of, you better walk into that room like God sent you there.

Ever since, it's been playing on repeat in my mind. The first "room" I thought of when I saw that quote was my approach to writing this book. Am I walking into *this room* like I know God sent me? When I began this project, it was as clear as if God walked into my house, sat down at my kitchen table, and said to me, "It's time to write this book, Kristina. Now sit down, do it, and get rid of everything in your life that's standing in the way. Walk away from this, close the door on that, and do the work I'm telling you to do." And yet, sometimes I have the audacity to treat this task like it's optional. Sometimes, I get worried and fearful about social media and caught up in "What will people think?!"

It's ridiculous, actually, because I'm very confident in the fact that writing this book is part of God's plan for me – but am I walking into this room like God sent me here? The best I could come up with is "Well ... sometimes."

Today, I want to encourage us both to walk into the rooms God sends us into with the confidence of someone who has been redeemed and called "mine" by God.

This can apply to motherhood, as well, ya know?

Mama, have you walked into the room like God sent you there?

Sometimes I think about Mary, the mother of Jesus, and I wonder what she must have felt as Jesus' mom. She was chosen out of everyone in the whole world, and I've always assumed her to be a gentle, humble, patient, and kind woman, but I'm sure there were times when she was overwhelmed, frustrated, or out of patience. I'm sure her husband did things that drove her crazy. Do you think Jesus tested the limits like our kids do? I don't know. But I do know that God told Mary to walk into a specific room – to be the earthly mother of the Savior of the world – and she had to walk in there with some conviction, with some strength, with purpose. She *knew* God chose her. He sent an angel to tell her so.

Nowadays, we don't hear much about God sending angels to relay messages – we have the Holy Spirit, which is something they didn't have yet. Knowing what God wants us to do, oftentimes requires that we spend time in the presence of the Lord. The lines of communication must be open. The tasks and purposes God has for us don't always come with trumpets blaring or the flapping of angel wings.

How do we know the things God wants us to do? How do we know what our gifts are? How do we know what room God is telling us to walk into?

Well, simply put, we won't - if we don't talk to God about it. So, talk to Him about it.

Sometimes, we get caught up in worrying about what makes us *feel* undeserving or unqualified. For me, I don't always feel like I'm good enough to write a devotion. I'm a new student of the Bible, I have no writing degree, and I've spent so much time living away from God. Often, I feel certain that someone else could do a better job; surely there's someone better and more qualified ... but that's what I love about our key verse for today. We are redeemed, ransomed, His.

Let's look again at the entire verse, and this time, I want you to really let the words sink in. Let them wash over you and empower you and inspire you.

There's a room you're being told to walk into.

Maybe it's motherhood, maybe it's motherhood *and* something else. Whatever it is, know that the Lord is telling you these three things:

- Don't be afraid.
- You are worthy of this calling.
- He calls you by name and says you are His.

I'll leave with you two different prompts to choose from today. Circle the one you're choosing and fill up these journal pages talking to God about the room He is sending you into.

Lord, I know you've told me to (insert assignment) _____ but am I doing it like I know You assigned it to me? The best answer I can come up with is "sometimes" and I know that's not good enough. Help me to carry out the tasks and acts of service You've placed on my heart and designed for me ...

God, I don't know what it is I'm supposed to be doing. I want to serve You, I want to follow You, I want my life to reflect You and point other people to You – but I don't know how, and I don't know what You want me to do. Help me know. Help me find a way to use my gifts and talents to serve You. Help me discover what my spiritual gifts are so that I can better ...

Day 28:

 All of Me

Psalm 25:1 NKJV

To You, O Lord, I lift up my soul.

This verse.

It's simple.

Short.

It is easy to gloss over and not think much about it, but everything in the Bible "is inspired by God and is useful to teach us what is true and to make us realize what is wrong in our lives. It corrects us when we are wrong and teaches us to do what is right. God uses it to prepare and equip his people to do every good work" (2 Timothy 3:16-17 NLT). So even our teensy tiny little key verse today has something for us.

"To you, O Lord, I lift up my soul" is my favorite verse in the Bible. I'm thrilled to be sharing it with you and smiling as I write about it. When I read it, I think about what it means to lift up my *soul.*

So, what does that mean?

This verse was written by King David, an imperfect man who loved God. He chose an interesting set of words here, didn't he? He could have said a lot of things other than soul.

This psalm could have said...

To you, O Lord, I lift up my time.

To you, O Lord, I lift up my heart.

To you, O Lord, I lift up my mind.

To you, O Lord, I lift up myself.

To you, O Lord, I lift up my finances.

To you, O Lord, I lift up my schedule.

To you, O Lord, I lift up my circumstances.

To you, O Lord, I lift up my troubles.

To you, O Lord, I lift up my anxieties.

To you, O Lord, I lift up my prayers.

To you, O Lord, I lift up my _____.

But it says soul.

Soul encompasses everything – everything we could think to lift up, and everything that would never even cross our minds. Soul is so much more than the pieces, it's the sum.

Soul is, quite literally, the only thing we take with us when we die.

In the rest of Psalm 25, David goes on to spill out his soul to God in the form of beautiful poetry. He asks God to direct his paths, asks God to forget the stupid things he did when he was younger. He glorifies God with his words and talks about the respect and fear he has for Him. He asks God to rescue him from the troubles of his heart and pledges to wait on God.

Isn't that everything?

Think about your own life – as a wife, mom, friend, daughter, sister, in-law, employee, whatever. Is there any part of your life that wouldn't fall into one of these categories? David lifted up his *entire soul* to God and left nothing untouched, no stone unturned. That's what God wants from us, too. It's what He wants from you. He wants *it all.*

He desires more than five rushed minutes with you in the morning. He wants more than just a ritual. He wants you to give Him more than just checking off something from a list. He wants more than just a little piece of you. He wants all of you. He wants your soul. What does that mean to you?

Of course, when we became Christians, we surrendered our souls, but is it something we continue to do? Giving my heart and soul to God and inviting Jesus into my life as my Savior, isn't the same thing as offering up my soul to Him every day. (And if I'm being honest, I don't do it every day. But shouldn't I strive to?)

So how do we do that? What does that look like?

The first thing that comes to mind is the command to pray without ceasing. If we are lifting up our souls, that is everything we have and every part of us, to God, don't you think it would include constant praying? 1 Thessalonians 5:16-18 NLT says, "Always be joyful. Never stop praying. Be thankful in all circumstances, for this is God's will for you who belong to Christ Jesus."

Romans 12:9-21 provides us with a list of Christian behaviors that we will look at tomorrow. The more scripture we plant within our hearts, the easier it will be to know what it looks like to live a life of submission to God – a life that lifts up our soul, *continuously*.

As a mom, sometimes it feels like everything about me is really all about everybody else. You spend so much time taking care of your family and there's not much time spent on yourself.

Maybe you're reading this and feeling like lifting up your soul to God is just another thing to handle, another thing to accomplish. God knows you. He knows your heart and your soul and your thoughts. But Him knowing isn't the same thing as having a relationship. He wants you to take everything to Him. As Mama, tender-of-children, we should understand better than anyone else the difference between knowing how our children feel versus our children coming to us for comfort. There's just something about being *that person* to my son that turns my guts to mush. I'm his safe place. I'm his home. He can count on me and find rest in my arms.

God wants the same thing for us, for His children. He wants us to run to Him. He wants us to know He is our safe place. He is where we can be raw, and real, and open, and honest. We can fling ourselves into His arms and trust Him to catch us.

Kids don't know how to be guarded like adults. They just *are* open and honest and deeply authentic – good or bad. You tend to always know where their souls stand because they just put it all out there, ya know? That's a good representation of what our relationship with God would look like if we made a habit of lifting up our souls to Him. Just having an open, messy, unashamed, whole-hearted love and devotion towards Him; releasing to Him every raw emotion; exhibiting total dependence in every facet of life.

> *As Mama, tender-of-children, we should understand better than anyone else the difference between knowing how our children feel versus our children coming to us for comfort.*

I wonder if that is part of what Jesus meant in Matthew 18 when He said we should become as little children if we want to enter the kingdom of heaven.

What area of your life do you struggle with turning over to God? What part of your soul isn't quite as "lifted up" as the rest? Give it to Him. Just hand it over, lift it up, lift all of *you* up. Don't make it complicated, don't feel pressured for it to be some perfect thing. Grand, messy action is a *fine* place to start.

Prayer Journal Prompt

To you, O Lord, I lift up my soul. Every part of it, starting today, even the parts that …

Day 29:

How To Be a Christian Mom

Romans 12:9-21 NLT

Don't just pretend to love others. Really love them. Hate what is wrong. Hold tightly to what is good. Love each other with genuine affection, and take delight in honoring each other. Never be lazy, but work hard and serve the Lord enthusiastically. Rejoice in our confident hope. Be patient in trouble, and keep on praying. When God's people are in need, be ready to help them. Always be eager to practice hospitality. Bless those who persecute you. Don't curse them; pray that God will bless them. Be happy with those who are happy, and weep with those who weep. Live in harmony with each other. Don't be too proud to enjoy the company of ordinary people. And don't think you know it all! Never pay back evil with more evil. Do things in such a way that everyone can see you are honorable. Do all that you can to live in peace with everyone. Dear friends, never take revenge. Leave that to the righteous anger of God. For the Scriptures say, "I will take revenge; I will pay them back," says the Lord. Instead, "If your enemies are hungry, feed them. If they are thirsty, give them something to drink. In doing this, you will heap burning coals of shame on their heads." Don't let evil conquer you, but conquer evil by doing good.

Before we can talk about how to be a Christian *mom*, it starts with how to be a Christian – and then "mamahood" is just tacked onto the end. There's a great list in Romans on how to behave like a Christian. In the margin of my journaling Bible, I've listed out the key words from this passage to make it easier for me to scan. It has become a reminder, or a checkup for my soul, whenever I see my notes.

In the box below, make your own notes or perhaps a bulleted list of the Christian traits and behaviors mentioned in our key passage of scripture. You can use the passage above or a different Bible translation of your preference.

These principles aren't as simple to live out as they are to list, are they? We know this well. But listing them out is a good place to start. Perhaps next we can ask God to hide His words in our hearts so that living out these traits become easier and easier.

I don't know about you, but I love a good list. So, now we have a list of what it looks like to behave as a Christian, how can we apply that to motherhood?

One thing I have learned in my journey of reading scripture and applying it to motherhood is that the stronger our faith, the better off we will be in every aspect of our lives – including, of course, the way we fill those "mama" shoes.

Today I will leave you with a list of questions to think about. And you can trust that I'm spending some time pondering these as well.

In what ways do I fail to love my child sincerely? Does this overlap with the mentality of "Do as I say, not as I do?"

Do I ever display evil or an acceptance of evil before my child, or is *every* form of evil hated in our house? Do I demonstrate right or wrong? Am I a successful gatekeeper in keeping out evil in the forms of who or what I invite into my home, what I allow to happen in my home, what I watch and listen to in my home, and the tones and words I use in my home?

Does my child receive enough affection – both physical and spiritual? Am I encouraging? Do I give enough praise? Do I slow down and give enough cuddles and love?

Do I put my needs last – giving preference to my child or each of my children?

Do my children see me excited, diligent, and eager to serve the Lord? Do they see me cheerfully serving them, serving my family, serving my church, serving my community, serving my friends, serving strangers?

Do my children witness me praying? Worshipping?

Is my home a place of hospitality? Are my children growing up in an environment that demonstrates what it means to be hospitable?

When I feel wronged by my child, how do I respond to them? How do my children see me respond to family or friends (or even strangers) who I feel have wronged me? Do they see me bless them?

Am I happy when my child is happy? Am I sad when my child is sad? Do I validate their emotions, or do I try to "fix" them or explain them away? Do I shame my child for the feelings they feel, or do I offer support and comfort? Do my children see me as an example of being a good friend to others?

Am I humble? Am I willing to learn? Do I spend enough time in the Word of God in front of my children, gleaning as much as I can and applying what I read to my life? Or do I rely on my own opinions instead of God's truths? Am I teachable or am I stuck in my own "truths?"

How do I respond to evil?

Do I live a life of peace? In what ways do I strive to create a peaceful home? Do I demonstrate to my child(ren) a spirit of revenge or a spirit of submission to God and His right to avenge and judge evil?

Do I overcome evil with good?

Those are loaded questions. As I read through this passage of scripture and asked myself each of these questions; let me tell you I felt chills all over my body, time after time. I won't give you a prayer journal prompt. Today, I will give you plenty of space to talk to God and follow the leadings of the Holy Spirit. Listen as he leads you to be a Christian mother. Be humble as He speaks to you about areas of your life you may need to deal with.

God bless this time of prayer.

Day 30:

Losing My Mind

Ephesians 4:22-24 NIV

You were taught, with regard to your former way of life, to put off your old self, which is being corrupted by its deceitful desires; to be made new in the attitude of your minds; and to put on the new self, created to be like God in true righteousness and holiness.

Have you ever said to your kids (or maybe just though it in your brain), "I'm about to lose my mind?!"

I'm guilty.

Some days, mom life is wild, right? More than once I've felt like I'm losing my ever-loving mind. Between cleaning up the same messes and repeating the same words, the days start to blur together, and I get to the point where I'm just ready for a change!

Honestly, days that have me feeling like I'm about to lose my mind are the days when I feel the most lost in motherhood. The hectic days when everything is going wrong; and the house is noisy, and messy, and dirty, and I'm getting minimal cooperation at every turn. The days when it feels like I'm just going against the grain on a team all by myself. The days where I have to be "stern mommy" and the moments when stern mommy turns into angry mommy. The days that, honestly, just aren't that great and I start thinking *this is not how I want to spend my time!*

That's when I start to feel lost again, because it feels like I'm totally out of control and I'm spending my time in ways I'd really rather not. The day is not going according to plan, and life just isn't how I pictured it! I know you've felt that way. Feeling lost in motherhood isn't always about feeling like you've lost part of yourself along the way, or feeling like you've lost hobbies, interests, or free time. Sometimes feeling lost in motherhood is feeling like you're losing your mind; because you've lost control of the day; and you've lost control of the plan and you've lost the ability to choose to have a good day somewhere along the way.

I don't know about you, but I am a morning person. I was chatting with a friend recently and she asked if I was a morning person. I told her that I wake up like a ping pong ball. She said she was jealous and always wished she woke up like a Pop Tart. That's me! And then I told her I've always been like this.

Meanwhile my husband is the morning sludge in our house, bless his heart. He is! He's a morning grump, and it's just one of the many ways we are opposites. I always tell him he has to wake up and choose to be happy, ya gotta choose to have a good day. To which he grumpily cuts his eyes at me from across the steaming coffee mugs.

Even though I am the type of person who wakes up bouncing off the walls, and eager to enjoy another great day, sometimes I find myself in the middle of a not-so-great-day. My happy little ping-pong ball ways can turn grumpy. It's not that I'm annoyed or bothered by being a mom – it's that I would have chosen a different motherhood experience for the day, like I would have chosen the fun things and the good, rewarding, cherishable parts of motherhood. Some days I get the *other* parts. I can think back to when my son was two and three years old and he is refusing to eat his breakfast (that I prepared knowing that he likes,) and throwing a fit for snacks, and not playing nice with his toys, making a huge mess, throwing temper tantrums over every minor inconvenience, not cooperating as I'm trying to do some basic chores, and the list goes on! Some days were just *like that,* and right in the middle of a day that a few hours ago, I had popped out of bed and chosen contentment, I find myself quite discontent.

So, what do we do? How do we handle it, Mama?

As we end our time together in this book, it seems like a fine time to introduce you to the format of my next devotion, which involves less storytelling and more walks through the Bible together. Open your Bible now to Ephesians 4:1, and we're going to take a little walk through some points brought out in the 4th and 5th chapters that are just *too good*. I believe these insights will really help you in your motherhood walk.

The very first verse of Ephesians tells us to walk worthy of our callings. Let it wash over you right now that you were called to motherhood by the Artist who created you *and* created your child or your children. It was a match made in Heaven. You were crafted, chosen, and called – and Paul, who wrote the book of Ephesians, is reminding you (and me) right now that we better act right. Have you ever said that to your kids? "You better act right!" Paul is telling us the same thing.

> *Let it wash over you right now that you were called to motherhood by the Artist who created you and created your child.*

I can imagine the advice translating into something an old, southern grandma might say. "You better mother those kids like the good Lord picked you for the job and not all willy-nilly like the things we do and say don't matter, because they do!" But oh, man, it's hard! How do we do that? It's one thing to tell us to walk worthy, but how? Where do we ever start?

Well, next up, Paul tells us exactly how. I love Paul for giving us a list. I'm such a list girl.

In verses 2-4 in chapter 4, Paul reminds us to walk worthy of the calling to which we were called. That calling is us displaying:

- humility
- gentleness
- patience
- tolerance
- love
- peacefulness
- pointing others to God

Wait, did he just describe a good mama, or did he just describe a good mama?!

Next, he spends some time talking about spiritual gifts and how each Christian is given a gift, why we're given gifts, how long we should use our gifts, and why it matters. I won't go into that right now because we will study it in depth in the next devotional, but for now, let's move down to verse 14. I love how he talks about children in verse 14.

Anytime the Bible mentions children, it speaks directly to my soul as a mother.

Verse 15, we're instructed to speak truth in love.

That's something that moms can sometimes have a hard time finding balance in – I know I struggle with that! As a stay-at-home-mom, most of the discipline and instruction comes from me, because I am the one who's with our son the most. It can be hard to speak the truth in love when it's a rough day or a particularly upsetting moment or circumstance.

But in verses 17 through 24, we're reminded that we are called to be different. We're to be different from the world and different from our old selves.

What a beautiful reminder, and what a lovely way to remind us, that different is not bad, different does not mean lost. In fact, it's part of God's design for our lives!

How can we actually *be* different, though? Life looks nothing like the way it did before becoming mama, but what's the *correct* way to be different? What is God's way of being different? Following His design for change is key.

Paul gives us another list. Way to go, Paul!

Mama, read verses 25 through 32 and make your own list of what Paul (and God) is telling you to put away.

Chapter 5 begins with telling us how to walk in love, how to walk in light, and how to walk in wisdom – all are so important for mamas to do. We are optimally poised and positioned to be the first people pointing our children to Jesus.

Verse 1 of chapter 5 says we should imitate God like children imitate. Write down a funny story or a funny thing your child does that is an imitation of someone or something. This book and the prayer journal sections may end up being precious to you later in life, and how wonderful would it be to have tucked into the pages a precious memory of your child?

I know there are times, maybe even days, when you feel like you are losing your mind. But there is always hope.

Not losing our minds can be just as simple as focusing in on these two things:

- ❋ The behaviors God wants us to demonstrate.
- ❋ The joys of motherhood tucked into even difficult moments.

Nothing is all bad. Some days we just need to take a deep breath and push past the moments that make us feel like we're losing something – losing our minds, losing the day, losing ourselves. God has given us His entire book, His Holy Word, that tells us what to do and how to do it. Praise God from Whom all blessings flow that we have this help. Otherwise, we might really (and actually) be lost.

God, thank You for deep breaths and reminders to focus on You and to focus on the good. Some days I feel like I'm losing my mind, and that makes me feel like I've lost any resemblance of a good life, but I know that's not true. Help me to step fully into the righteousness and holiness I was created by You to embody, in my life as your daughter, and as a mother to some of Your other children. Remind me in the difficult moments that You are with me. Remind me of who I am in You. Remind me of the calling You've placed on my life, especially when it feels like I am losing my mind. Right now, I want to pray about …

Acknowledgements

First and foremost, God gets all of the glory. As I was finishing up the book, I came across this verse, "My lips shall utter praise, For You teach me Your statutes" (Psalm 119:171 NKJV). I paused and thought about the "full-circleness" of this project that has consumed so much of my life over the past few years. Inspiration for this book began in the pages of my Bible and my prayer journal. As I leaned so heavily on God through my own struggles with motherhood and identity and the callings on my life right now, God taught me His statutes. From there, sprouted praise. And from there, I knew I had to help other mamas find that, too. When we are rooted in Him, we will bloom. Praise God from Whom *all* blessings flow. I am so grateful that He wants to use me. I am so grateful that He saved me. I will never be able to repay Him for the ways He has blessed me or for the sacrifice of sending Jesus, His son – but using what He has given me to bring Him glory is how I plan to spend the rest of my life.

I also want to thank my family for supporting me – with you, this wouldn't have been possible.

To my husband, Alan – I think back on the years we've spent together and just marvel at the way God can use anything and anyone. We've come so far from the people we were when we met. You have loved so many versions of me, and for that, I am grateful, humbled, and proud to be your wife. Thank you for loving me so completely, and for being supportive through my path toward becoming a true author. I love you.

To my children – affectionally known in my heart as Biscuit and Lottie Lou. You two will never understand the way your mere existence has changed me down to the core. You make me better, and one of my greatest aspirations is to be worthy of the love you so freely give to me as your "Mama." I love you both so tremendously. Without you, this book would not have been written. You are woven into the pages of this book and my own story, and I'm grateful for the way God has used my experiences so far as your mama to be a window into the love the Father has for His children. You will forever be my greatest accomplishment.

To both of my parents and all of my grandparents and the countless people whose prayers have carried me and protected me all throughout my life. I don't know where I would be without your love and guidance and constant presence.

To my own Momma – to whom this book is dedicated. The way you encouraged me and helped watch my children during this process, the way you heard my concerns and comforted me through the doubts and insecurities I faced will never be forgotten. This book grew from a seed planted in Sunday School – a place I would not have been if not for your influence in and on my life. The leader asked, "Who is the strongest Christian you know?" And I thought of you and knew in that instant that I wanted to be that for my children, too. I knew the kind of mom I wanted to be because of the type of mother you have always been to me. Thank you for that gift.

To my Daddy, the person responsible for so many of the things that make me "me," both good and bad. You imparted on me a drive and an entrepreneurial spirit I couldn't have done this without. You make me feel understood when I take on a new adventure or endeavor, or sometimes a little of both. You even wanted to read my book – a book for moms, and I never have to wonder if you're proud of me because you show it in so many ways. Thank you for being a source of constant love and making me feel normal for my entire life.

To my sister – all of my life, I wanted to write, but it wasn't until I wrote a children's book about you that I found myself actually writing. Thank you for always being my sound board and partner in social media, for always being ready to hold the camera or brainstorm with me, and for always laughing with me, not at me. I am so grateful to call you not just my sister, but a friend.

To all of my friends who covered this book in prayer and encouraged me in their own unique ways – thank you for being my pillars. Especially Brittany, Jennifer, and Kerri. You three are my true "Mama-Sister-Friends" and every mama on the planet deserves to have friends like each of you have been to me.

To the Found Mama Club members – my very first readers. Thank you for joining me on this journey, for trusting me, and for being a part of this. You gave me courage and increased my boldness to continue. A sincerest thank you to Darla B., Doremi G., Brandy G., Lara G., Brittany C., Emily B., Elisabeth W., Charity C., Kerri H., Rebecca G., Karyn W., Missy K., Olivia W., Joy R., Chelsea C., Jodi D., Sandra E., Stasha N., Kylie V., Delia S., Catherine K., Chelsey J., Amber B., Lauren W., Brooke M., Lindsay S., Tina W., Lisa V. Sarah S., Jessica R., Becky P., Grace F., Cristine H., V Owen, Miranda G., Ruth G., Megan I., Erin M., Tessa K., Nicole B., Morgan G., Elaine B., Maria V., Roblin F., Joe G, Mary C., Lindsey P., Lori C., Kristen R., Kristyn W., Chrissy T., Vanessa P., Ashley S., Kelsy D., Kate M., Lori G., Elizabeth M., and Angela B. I prayed often for each of you, by name, and will always be grateful for your partnership. Several of you, and you know who you are, went above and beyond in encouraging me along this path and walking this journey with me, and I will never forget your kindness.

And finally, to my editor, Mrs. Karyn. You joined this cause when it was still being formed, and you've

been so much more than "just" an editor. You've
been a friend, secret-keeper, shoulder to cry on,
encourager, source of strength, and my biggest
cheerleader. I am blessed to call you my dear friend,
a bestie, "wonderous expert", and a soul sister. No
amount of thanks for the work you have put into this
will ever be adequate. So, I will publicly repeat an
offer I once made to you and say, I would be honored
to return the favor one day. I love you and your kind
and tender heart — and from the bottom of my heart,
thank you.

Daily To-Do List Free Download

As a special thank-you, I want to gift you a free digital download of this to-do list, or a different style of your choosing. Follow the steps below to access your free download-and-print to-do list.

1. Visit my website:

www.authorkristinabrooks.com/category/all-products

2. Add one of the digital download to-do lists to your cart.

3. At checkout, use the coupon code "NOTLOST"

Coupon code valid once per customer. Please do not share this code with others.

About the Author

Kristina is a wife to Alan and mother to Seabastian and Charlotte. She left the corporate world in 2019 to stay home with their firstborn and the rest, as they say, is history.

Those closest to Kristina know she enjoys a simple life but are not at all surprised when she tells them she's trying something new.

She previously wrote and illustrated a children's book, *The Princess Who Lost Her Crown.*

The Found Mama is her debut devotional series, with more coming soon!

Connect with Kristina as she shares her never-ending projects, adventures, and encouragement:

www.authorkristinabrooks.com

www.facebook.com/authorkristinabrooks

Instagram: @authorkristinabrooks

TikTok: @authorkristinabrooks

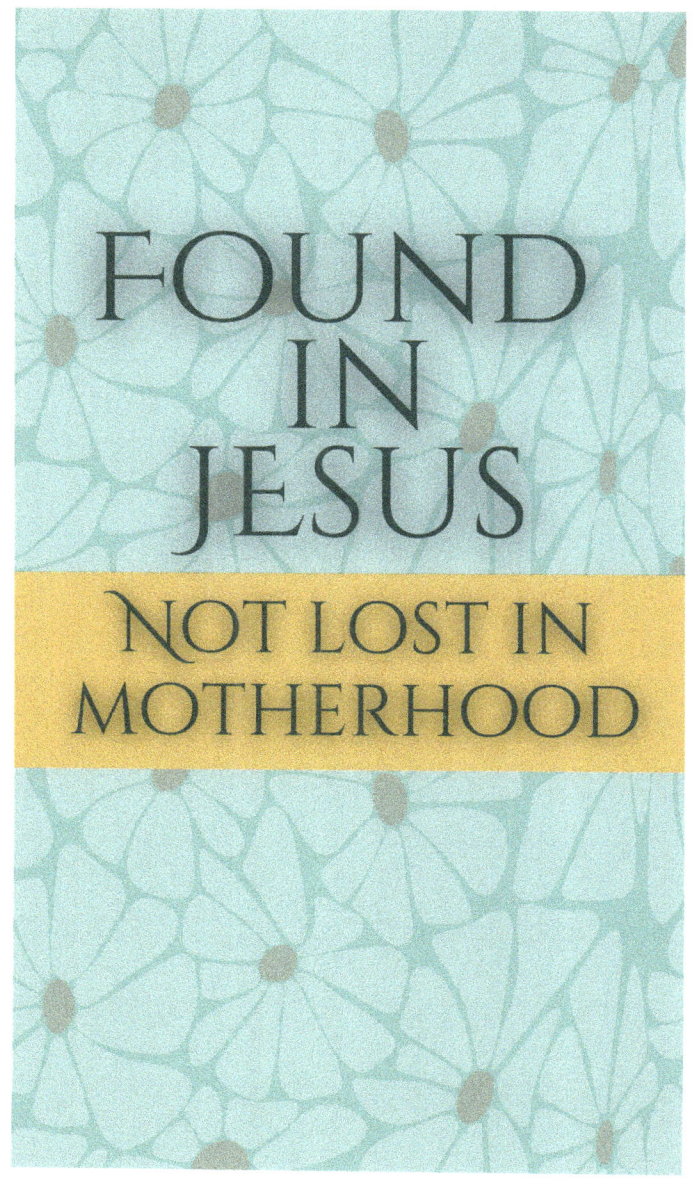

Found in
Jesus,
Not Lost in
Motherhood

www.ingramcontent.com/pod-product-compliance
Lightning Source LLC
Chambersburg PA
CBHW050446150626
46551CB00029B/1795